The 8 Ste_ _ _ _ _ _ _ Advantage:

How to Increase Sales in Your Restaurant

By: Christopher Hallenbeck

Great Point Publishing

Gloversville, NY

The 8 Step Upselling Advantage:
How to Increase Sales in Your Restaurant
By: Christopher Hallenbeck

To order additional copies of this title, contact your favorite local bookstore or visit *www.greatpointpublishing.com*

Paperback ISBN: 978-1-7333797-4-8

Cover design by: Gareth Bobowski

Book design by: Christopher Hallenbeck

Printed in the United States of America

**Published by: Great Point Publishing, LLC.
Gloversville, NY**

Dedicated to Mary Jo and Cubby Faville

In thanks and appreciation for the

opportunity to develop and hone the skills

and strategies presented within.

TABLE OF CONTENTS

Dear Restaurant Owners and Managers,

Welcome to <u>The 8 Step Upselling Advantage</u>. This book is the first book in a series developed for the restaurant industry to help restaurant owners, managers, and employees increase sales and improve service. It helps people just like you.

First, the readers, both restaurant owners/managers and restaurant employees, are greeted with an introduction letter explaining how this book can help them. Next, in chapter one, you (and your staff/colleagues) will learn how to be great at sales. Chapter two follows and explains how <u>The 8 Step Upselling Advantage</u> works. Chapter three builds on the previous chapters, teaching you how to upsell with the <u>The 8 Step Upselling Advantage</u>. Chapter four provides scripts and formula explanations of the eight step upselling advantage, helping you understand the system taught. Chapter five presents you with a troubleshooting guide, so you're able to learn from mistakes and how to remedy them. Next, chapter six introduces our fictional character Bill and his journey of how he read this book, worked at a restaurant, and how he applied the techniques learned from the eight step upselling advantage in his career as a sales engineer. Chapter seven follows up with more tips to help you learn the eight step upselling advantage faster and easier. Last, chapter eight teaches you the best place to learn The 8 Step Upselling Advantage.

When your employees are reading <u>The 8 Step Upselling Advantage</u>, they will learn that everything they need to begin their careers already exists in your establishment. They will also learn that you're providing them with the tools they need to accomplish the goal of having a successful career, whether it be with your establishment or with multiple organizations. The skills and lessons taught in this book apply to many careers and are especially helpful to your employees who hope to break into the sales world. (Note: In the next section, "Dear Restaurant

Employees..." the readers will learn of job opportunities that the skills taught in this book could help them earn if they learn the 8 Step Upselling Advantage and utilize these skills in your restaurant).

After reading The 8 Step Upselling Advantage and applying the techniques and strategies taught inside this book, the employee will then have the tools they need that could help them advance their future careers. When the employee utilizes this resource you've provided, this benefits your establishment through increased sales and an improvement of customer service.

I hope that the strategies within this book help increase sales in your restaurant, and improve service. After reading The 8 Step Upselling Advantage, I'd like to invite you to check out my website increaserestaurantsales.com where you can learn more tips, and strategies all focused on helping you continue to increase sales in your restaurant, helping you continue to improve service to your patrons, and other useful information all developed to help you to continue to operate a successful establishment. Also, don't forget to sign up for our free email newsletter while you're there so you can continue to learn the latest strategies and opportunities all developed to help you and your restaurant, and also let you know when future books in this series are released. Thanks again for reading The 8 Step Upselling Advantage, I wish you the best of luck!

Next, let's look at how reading The 8 Step Upselling Advantage benefits both your employees and your restaurant in the next introduction letter, "Dear Bartenders, Servers, and Staff... How this book can help advance your career".

Dear Bartenders, Servers, and Staff...
How this book can help advance your career

Welcome to <u>The 8 Step Upselling Advantage</u>. This book is the first book in a series developed for the restaurant industry to help you learn how to upsell and, in turn, increase sales in your restaurant or pizzeria.

    <u>The 8 Step Upselling Advantage</u> can also help you begin developing and honing skills that could be beneficial to you further in the future of your career. The strategies you're going to learn from reading this book and then applying these techniques in a restaurant could lead to better career opportunities for you. This transition is definitely not easy, but it definitely is not impossible. This book teaches you how you can make the transition. Let's look at where you might be now and how you can improve opportunities to advance your career....

    In September 2018, a writer named Betsy Verecky wrote an article for thestacker.com titled "Worst jobs in America". The list was compiled "using data from Payscale and The Bureau of Labor Statistics, Stacker surveyed 500 occupations to come up with 50 jobs that have the highest job misery index."[1]

    Included in this list are jobs associated with the restaurant industry; in fact, jobs associated with the restaurant and food industry accounted for over 20% of the 50 jobs listed. Here is a list of where some of these jobs ranked: Bartender #45, Host/Hostesses #42, Waiters/Waitresses #36, Combined food preparation and serving workers (including fast food) #34. Counter attendants for cafeterias, food concessions, and coffee shops #33, Retail Salespersons #31, Driver/Sales workers #22.[1]

    This list might be slightly depressing to you, or you might be reading it and saying to yourself that you do not believe it, as right now, you love your job being a waiter/waitress or working in a different position within the restaurant industry. "Still, it's an industry with high turnover. Only 5% of waiters and waitresses have spent 20 years or more on the job."[1]

Operators even acknowledge that hiring and keeping employees is tough but not impossible. "I hire people at an entry level," says Paul Giannone, founder of Paulie Gee's in Brooklyn, New York. "I don't hire a dishwasher who wants to be a dishwasher. I hire a dishwasher who wants to be a pizza maker. They end up working harder because they want to move up to being a pizza maker."[2]

This is the same attitude you should display at your restaurant or pizzeria job. To paraphrase Mr. Giannone, you need to work hard because you want to move up.

We talked about some of the worst jobs in America. Now, let's talk about some of the best jobs in America.

Every year, the website glassdoor.com publishes a list of the "50 best jobs in America". In their recent article "50 Best Jobs in America for 2019", among the best jobs in America for 2019 included #13 – Sales Manager whose median based salary is $65,000/year, and also #14 – Sales Engineer whose median based salary is listed at $90,000/year. [3]

The Glassdoor Team also posted an article - "Top Jobs for Sales Professionals". According to glassdoor.com, "If you're looking for a job that pays well, has tremendous room for growth and requires an unbeatable drive, consider a career in sales. Motivated, yes, by the bottom line as well as a passion for customers and employees, sales leaders truly make a business run." [4]

Some of the top jobs for sales professionals that were included in this list were: Sales Development Representative, Account Executive, Outside Salesperson, Sales Insight Analyst, Account Manager, Sales Engineer, Sales Enablement Manager, Sales Manager, Director of Sales, and Vice President of Sales.[4]

The structure of this book is outlined specifically along this same scenario, showing you by example potentially how to go from "the worst job" to applying yourself and earning "the best job".

The structure of this book is formatted as follows: First the readers, both restaurant owners/managers and restaurant employees, are greeted with an introduction letter explaining how this book can help them. Next, in chapter one, you will learn how to be great at sales. Chapter two follows and explains to you how the eight step upselling advantage works. Chapter three builds on the previous chapters, teaching you how to upsell with the eight step upselling advantage. Chapter four provides you with scripts and formula explanations of the eight step upselling advantage, helping you understand even more fully the system taught. Chapter five presents you with a trouble shooting guide, so you're able to learn from mistakes and how to remedy them. Next, chapter six introduces to you our fictional character Bill and his journey of how he read this book, started working at a restaurant, and how he applied the techniques learned from the eight step upselling advantage in his career as a sales engineer. Chapter seven follows up with more tips to help you learn the eight step upselling advantage faster and easier. Last, chapter eight teaches you the best place to learn The 8 Step Upselling Advantage.

In closing, I hope you find, while reading this book, it helps you see similar opportunities and scenarios you've experienced in the past, and through the 8 step upselling advantage, you will now learn how to turn those similar opportunities and scenarios into new successful sales experiences!

After reading this book and applying the techniques and strategies taught, I firmly believe you will have developed new skill sets that could potentially advance your future career.

Now, check out chapter one on the next page to begin learning about The 8 Step Upselling Advantage and your first lessons- How to Be Great at Sales!

Chapter 1

HOW TO BE GREAT AT SALES
Five Lessons that you need to learn now

The last decade has been nothing short of a roller coaster ride for operators in the restaurant and pizzeria industries. In 2009, nearly 65,000 pizza stores in the United States saw their total industry sales decrease by almost $359 million. Their pizza sales still totaled over $36 billion, with the average per-unit sales for all U.S. pizzerias equaling $558,671.00. However, in October 2010, pizzerias were starting to see a turnaround after 12 consecutive quarters of declining customer counts.[5]

Additionally, in the restaurant industry, according to an article published on the nation's restaurant news website in July 2010, "the number of restaurants in the United States has fallen by 5,204 units, a 1-percent decline from the total number of eateries recorded in spring of 2009, according to the NPD."[6]

Today, pizza sales in the United States are up $45 billion dollars (in 2018 compared to data from 2017). Also, average unit sales are estimated at $577,909, which is an increase of $19,238 when compared to the figures taken from 2009.[2] "On top of that, consumers are now spending as much money eating out as they do eating at home. According to a recent study in Consumer Reports, around half of every food dollar is spent at restaurants, equaling roughly $2,222 per person, per year."[2]

This, of course, is positive and encouraging news. But there are still areas that are lacking, and that should be of concern to all of us. For example, a recent survey of 68,950 restaurant-goers told *Consumer Reports* that nothing matters more in the choice of a restaurant than the taste and quality of the food. According to *Consumer Reports,* "And while respondents were satisfied with about half of the restaurants listed in the survey, they did note areas that needed improvement such as, service that was lacking, restaurants that were too noisy, inattentive waiters, and long waits to order and get the check." [1]

I'd like to focus on two takeaways from that quote above, specifically when it tells us that "service that was lacking" and "inattentive waiters."

I believe that you care about your job, and the fact that you're reading this book tells me you want to better yourself and have pride in your work. I also believe that, together, we can help improve the customer service and experience at your restaurant while increasing revenue for the establishment.

This book is going to teach you two ways to accomplish these goals. The first way is through teaching you how to be great at sales. The second way is showing you how to learn the skill of upselling on the phone or in person as a server, bartender, or delivery driver.

During my experiences in the food industry, I have tried experimenting with different sales techniques to develop an upselling strategy that could easily be taught, learned, and used successfully by anyone who wanted to put the time and practice into mastering the skill and procedure. The technique I'm about to teach you is a result of my trials and errors.

The 8 Step Upselling Advantage was developed in live everyday restaurant scenarios in person and on the phone. It will be successful not only in increasing business sales, but it will also be instrumental in increasing your efficiency as an employee. By increasing your efficiency as a server, whether you are a waiter, waitress, bartender, or driver, I believe we can help combat critiques such as "service that was lacking" and "inattentive waiters.

The first thing you need to learn to accomplish this goal, though, is learning how to be great at sales.

Lesson One.
You Need to Learn How to Make Money.

The first lesson in learning how to be great at sales is learning how to make money. Some of the best advice I have ever learned about sales in the food industry, and how to be great at sales in general, comes from a lesson I learned a few years ago while I was listening to a recording by Earl Nightingale entitled "The Strangest Secret."

This lesson will be extremely important and helpful to you, as you will be referencing it either directly or indirectly every time your phone rings or a patron visits your establishment. I frequently still listen to "The Strangest Secret" as the lessons it contains are still valuable, fresh, and influential today, just as they first were when they were recorded in 1956.

In 1956, Earl Nightingale wrote and recorded a message that was to be played to a small group of salesmen during his absence. Earl entitled his message "The Strangest Secret." Shortly after his primary audience heard the recording, many began requesting copies of "The Strangest Secret" to be played for their friends and family. So, Earl arranged for duplication of his message by Columbia Records, and much to Earl's surprise, this recording would eventually go on to sell over a million records, earning Earl Nightingale a gold record.[7]

Today, over 60 years later, Earl's message is still referenced and applicable to our modern world. While some of the data originally presented may be outdated, "The Strangest Secret" contains some of the best advice I have ever learned about the pizza and restaurant industry. This advice will be extremely important and helpful to you as well, today and in the future. Additionally, all of you will be applying its principles every time you make a sale, every time you fail to make a sale, and as you teach it to your employees. The lesson Earl teaches us is this:

"You know most men will tell you that they want to make money without understanding the law. The only people who make money work in the Mint. The rest of us must earn money. This is what causes those who keep looking for something for nothing, or a free ride to fail in life. The only way to earn money is by providing people with services or products which are needed and useful. We exchange our product or service for the other man's money. Therefore, the law is that our financial return will be in direct proportion to our service. Success is not the result of making money. Making money is the result of success. And success is in direct proportion to our service. Most people have this law backwards. They believe that you're successful if you earn a lot of money. The truth is you can only earn money if you're successful ... Once this law is fully understood, any thinking person can tell his own fortune. If he wants more, he must be of more service to those from whom he receives his return. If he wanted less, he only has to reduce this service. This is the price that you must pay for what you want." [7]

This is precisely what you need to be striving for as an employee or as an owner or manager who is teaching your employees every day how to do their job the best they can.

The most important thing you need to understand and truly believe while they are learning how to upsell and working in your establishment is that *"the only way to earn money is by providing people with services or products which are needed and useful."* [7]

In short, you are simply showing people how your establishment's services "are needed and useful" and how it will make your patron's world a better place.

Lesson Two.

You Need to Learn the Most Important Secret of Salesmanship.

On August 3, 1920, Frank Bettger walked into the offices of John Scott and Company, a large wholesale grocer in Philadelphia, Pennsylvania. Now, according to Dale Carnegie, Mr. Bettger was "one of the most successful and highest paid salesman in America" in the 1920s and '30s, and on this warm August morning in 1920, Frank Bettger walked into the offices of John Scott and Company as a salesman for Fidelity Mutual Life Insurance Company of Philadelphia. Mr. Bettger had one goal in mind: to sell John Scott a life insurance policy. Following up on a lead and wanting to introduce himself in person, Mr. Bettger found Mr. Scott that morning, but Mr. Scott had no time and no interest in talking about life insurance. He was 63 years old at the time and had stopped buying insurance years ago, but Mr. Bettger knew what questions to ask and when to ask them. Twenty minutes later, he found himself in John Scott's private office, and a short time after that, Mr. Scott wrote out a check and made a deposit that day of $8,672 to put his plan in action. Mr. Bettger later found out this was one of the biggest individual sales that had ever been made in their company's history, and a few weeks later, he was invited to tell this story at a national sales convention in Boston.

       Immediately following his talk at the convention, a man named Clayton M. Hunsicker approached Frank Bettger, shook his hand, and congratulated him on the sale. Then Mr. Hunsicker told Mr. Bettger something he soon learned was the most profound secret of dealing with people. Mr. Hunsicker said:

> *"I still doubt whether you understand exactly why you were able to make that sale."* [8]

Now, Mr. Hunsicker was a nationally known salesman and a man nearly twice the age of Frank Bettger, so eagerly and interested, Mr. Bettger replied:

"What do you mean?"[8]

Mr. Hunsicker then revealed to Frank Bettger the most vital truth he had ever heard about selling. So vital was this truth that, after hearing it, Frank Bettger resolved to dedicate the rest of his selling career to this principle. Mr. Hunsicker continued:

> *"The most important secret of salesmanship is to find out what the other fellow wants, then help him find the best way to get it. In the first minute of your interview with that man Scott, you took a blind stab, and accidentally found what he wanted. Then you showed him how he could get it. You kept on talking more about it, and asking more questions about it, never letting him get away from the thing he wanted. If you remember this one rule, selling will be easy."* [8]

By learning the most important secret of salesmanship, Frank Bettger now had a new form of inspiration, courage, and enthusiasm! This secret was something more than a new sales technique. To Frank Bettger, it was a philosophy to live by. He dedicated the rest of his career to:

"Finding out what people want and helping them get it." [8]

Lesson Three.
You Need to Learn How to Prepare the Sale to the Customer.

In Lesson Two, you read how Frank Bettger was successful in making one of the biggest sales in his company's history, and afterwards, you read Clayton Hunsicker's advice to Mr. Bettger. To complete this task, Mr. Bettger found what Mr. Scott wanted, and he helped him get it.

Afterwards, while presenting his advice to Mr. Bettger, Clayton Hunsicker explained how Mr. Bettger "took a blind stab, and accidentally found what he wanted ... showed him how he could get it ... kept on talking more about it ... asking more questions about it, never letting him get away from the thing he wanted." [8] That quote paraphrases how Frank Bettger was able to make the sale that day. But how exactly was Frank Bettger able to prepare the sale to Mr. Scott?

Recently, I attended a presentation by Howard Litwak, a Regional Director for Paradigm Associates, a national consulting firm, whose expertise includes "increasing sales and profitability."[9] Mr. Litwak also happens to be an amazing speaker and a Certified Business Coach. During his speech that night, Howard explained how to prepare and set up a successful sale.

> *"Building a sale is about creating value in the mind of the prospect. He/she needs to see that the benefits of doing business plus the cost of inaction outweighs the purchase price. Zig Ziglar has said that a prospect will not give you their big pile of money in exchange for a little pile of benefits. Effective questioning around benefits and consequences is the tool that the professional seller uses to create value. Although the prospect should feel that they are involved in a dialog, the seller is really directing a tactical conversation as there is specific information he/she needs to build a sale."* [10]

In the quote above, Howard is precisely explaining what Clayton Hunsicker taught Frank Bettger at the 1920 National Sales Convention in Boston. Through directing a tactical conversation, utilizing effective questioning, and creating value in the prospect's mind, Frank Bettger was able to prepare the sale to John Scott effectively and successfully.

Lesson Four.
You Need to Learn How to Present the Sale to the Customer.

Once you have prepared the sale to the customer through tactical conversation, effective questioning, and creating value in the prospect's mind, you are ready to present the sale. To present the sale to the customer effectively, remember Howard Litwak's advice: "Building a sale is about creating value in the mind of the prospect. He/she needs to see that the benefits of doing business plus the cost of inaction outweighs the purchase price." [10]

This is exactly how Frank Bettger was able to sell Mr. Scott the new life insurance policy. When Frank Bettger was first talking to John Scott, he asked Mr. Scott about his interests outside of his family and business, meaning charity, missionary, or religious work that Mr. Scott supported. Frank Bettger immediately followed this question with two more questions by asking Mr. Scott, "Did you ever consider that, when you die, your support will be withdrawn? Wouldn't this loss seriously handicap or even mean the discontinuance of some splendid work?" [8]

Just like Howard Litwak described in his advice above, through directing a tactical conversation, utilizing effective questioning, and creating value in the prospect's mind, Frank Bettger was able to prepare the sale to John Scott effectively and successfully. When Frank Bettger asked John Scott if he had any interests outside of his family and business, Frank Bettger learned that John Scott supported three foreign missionaries. Twenty minutes later, while in John Scott's private office, as a result of their conversation earlier, Frank Bettger was able to "build a sale by creating value in the mind of the prospect," just like Howard Litwak said would happen.

The new life insurance policy that John Scott bought that day wasn't to benefit his family or business; the beneficiaries on that policy were three foreign missionaries. Through this presentation by Frank Bettger, John Scott saw that the benefits of doing business with Frank Bettger that day - plus the cost of inaction - outweighed the purchase price. Again, like Howard Litwak described earlier, Mr. Bettger was able to prepare and present the sale successfully through tactical conversation, utilizing effective questioning, and creating value in the prospect's mind.

Lesson Five.
You Need to Learn How to Upsell to the Customer.

The final lesson on how to be great at sales is you need to learn how to upsell. So far, you've learned how to be great at sales, but this final lesson is going to teach you how to be really great at sales!

Upselling is a sales technique where you try to sell the customer either a separate, more profitable item, a product they might not have considered initially, or both. These add-ons or upgrades are an attempt to make a more profitable sale.

I've asked Rick Noel to explain more to you about why upselling is such a valuable skill to learn and how it is a skill that can benefit you for the rest of your career. Rick Noel is the CEO and founder of ebizroi.com, a successful internet marketing company, and has lots of experience as a successful salesman.

In just a moment, Rick will explain to you the importance of why you need to learn to upsell, how upselling provides numerous advantages for companies, and the benefits and values you'll gain from learning this skill. Now, here's Rick Noel:

"Thanks Chris! Hello everyone! Rick Noel here from ebizroi.com. Upselling is one of the most important skills that any successful

salesperson or sale force can master. The reason is simple. It is much easier and significantly less costly to upsell an existing customer than to acquire a brand new one. Let's examine why in more detail.

A typical path to purchase, whether Business to Business (B2B) or Business to Consumer (B2C), typically includes the following four stages: Awareness > Consideration >> Intent >>> Decision

For upselling, the **awareness** stage is rarely a barrier for existing customers. I say rarely because it is incumbent on sales and marketing to communicate effectively the capabilities of their products/services/offers, especially as their portfolio of offers evolves over time. If done deliberately, effective sales and marketing efforts can often short-circuit the awareness stage as existing customers know about the capabilities and ability of existing vendors to deliver.

Upselling provides companies an advantage in the **consideration** phase, since many aspects of the company are known from the pre-existing relationship. The upselling advantage in the consideration phase relies on past successful project deliveries with positive business outcomes.

 As buyers move into the **intent** phase of their path to purchase, having a pre-existing relationship with a vendor can have a strong influence on buyer's intent. During the intent phase, smart sales and marketing organizations will nurture their prospect's intent through carefully timed communications, offering unique insights into customer challenges, positioning solutions that uniquely address those challenges.

Oftentimes, in an upsell situation, the **decision** phase, which is when the buyer selects which vendor/solution to use, they will often favor those who have proven their value in past projects.

This makes the upsell purchase decision that much easier, removing risk of an unknown entity delivering a solution that can be critical to the buyer, their career, and their overall purchase experience.

In summary, it is always less costly to upsell an existing customer than to acquire a brand new one. Savvy businesses will look to grow revenue by upselling their existing customer base as aggressively or even more aggressively than their effort to grow revenue through new customer acquisition. When looking at the lifetime value of an existing customer, always be sure to factor in a strong upsell strategy to grow the business."[11]

Thanks Rick! Rick's wonderful explanation above covers why "upselling is one of the most important skills that any successful salesperson or sale force can master." [11] And how, when you factor in a strong upsell strategy to grow business, the decision increases the lifetime value of an existing customer; this is exactly how upselling can help you become really great at sales and how upselling can help you increase sales in your restaurant. Not only will learning how to upsell benefit you right now at your current establishment, but if you're entering the workforce as an employee in the food industry, learning how to upsell now can benefit your career in the future as you move on to other endeavors.

In the next chapter, you're going to learn about three more strategies that can help you. Afterwards, you'll learn the eight step upselling advantage formula, followed by a script analysis, and more strategies to help make sure you completely understand The 8 Step Upselling Advantage. Now, onto chapter two.

Chapter 2

THREE MORE STRATEGIES
to Help You

Now that you have learned the five lessons in how to be great at sales, here are three more strategies to help you as you learn more about The 8 step upselling advantage. In this chapter, we will identify and explain each of these strategies separately and then begin to build on teaching you how they all work together.

Strategy One.
Storytelling.

Williamsburg is a city in Virginia, which at one time served as the capital of the commonwealth from 1699 to 1780. Today, the city's tourism-based economy is driven by Colonial Williamsburg, the restored historic area of the city. Each year, more than four million tourists visit what is known as the historic triangle that consists of Williamsburg, Jamestown, and Yorktown. [12]

Part of the reason for the popularity is because Colonial Williamsburg takes visitors and transports them back in time to the dawn of America.[13] According to *tripadvisor.com*, the trip offers visitors the opportunity to engage with the local community and experience for themselves the daily struggles of wartime, and for that moment, they become a citizen of the Revolutionary City. A visit to the restored historic area is one of the top things to do in the city. [14, 15] However, despite all these interesting attractions, Colonial Williamsburg developed a major safety hazard that was a concern for many years.

Separating Colonial Williamsburg's Visitor's Center to enter into the historic district is the busy highway of Route 132Y. Due to increasing traffic, Route 132Y has become more hazardous to visitors who wanted to walk the historic area instead of taking a bus. Thankfully, in May 2002, an effort began to fix this problem, removing the hazard, making the experience safer, more convenient, and more enjoyable for visitors of the historic city.[16]

During roughly the next seven months, a $3 million, 500 foot pedestrian bridge, known as the "Bridge to The Past", was constructed over Route 132Y to provide safer and more convenient access for visitors to walk from the visitor's center into the historic area. To enhance safety further, the bridge was equipped with railings on each side. It also included benches for tourists who may need to rest. Plus, as the visitors walk along the bridge to the historic area, on the bridge's deck, there are engraved bronze plaques that help transition visitors back in time by illustrating what life was like during various time periods. For example, one plaque reads: "In 1954, you tolerated segregated schools." Another reads, in 1940, there was no television to watch. And on another, readers imagine life in 1776: "You were a subject of the king."[16]

In January 2003, a self-described history buff named Bob Fuhr was visiting Colonial Williamsburg and the newly built "Bridge to The Past."

Fuhr lives near Atlanta, GA. He is a Sales and Performance Consultant with Miller Heiman Group and the owner of North-South Enterprises.[16, 17, 18]

Fuhr utilizes his history knowledge as part of his sales scripts and strategies. He will usually open a presentation with a story about a famous battle, capturing the audience's attention with his storytelling skills. Then during the story, he will explain how this scenario is similar to a problem the group he is addressing is facing now. His vast business experience and expertise qualifies Fuhr to present sales and performance solutions and strategies to help the organization ultimately meet their goals. Fuhr will then weave the presentation towards a close with a description of the outcome of the same famous battle that he introduced in the beginning of the presentation or a different but similar and relevant famous event in history. Essentially, he teaches his audience that, through using similar strategies he discussed in the presentation, history repeats itself, and victory can be achieved by the organization, just like victory was the outcome from the historical perspectives that Fuhr presented throughout his sales performance presentation.

Fuhr is a master storyteller, and after nearly every presentation closing, the self-described history buff and sales and performance consultant is shown appreciation and approval through the sounds of a thunderous applause and sometimes even extended standing ovations. But what makes Fuhr's presentations so successful and in demand?

Part of the answer is that Fuhr's success is a result of the delivery of the strategies and advice, thanks to the combination of his business experience, presentations skills, and storytelling talents. Another reason why Fuhr's presentations are so successful is because they're similar to the storytelling strategies used by a man named Gerry Spence. Let's look at how Mr. Spence utilizes the effectiveness of storytelling in his work.

In 1929, Gerald "Gerry" Spence was born in Wyoming. 23 years later, in 1952, Spence graduated cum laude from the University of Wyoming Law School, and throughout his career, he developed a reputation and became known as the best trial lawyer for the people that ever existed.[19, 20,21]

The effectiveness of storytelling in your sales performance, just like inside the courtroom, can be described in the following quote. Gerry Spence once said, "a story is more magnetizing to the listener who feels his/her active participation will be necessary for the story to achieve its proper ending."[22]

Storytelling can be an effective technique and strategy to utilize in your sales performance. Regardless if you are presenting to a large audience, who are employed at a well-known organization, or a single customer while you are working as a server or bartender, a good story can help you earn the sale.

In lesson three from chapter one- how to be great at sales, you might recall that, in the lesson, Howard Litwak taught us that, "Although the prospect should feel that they are involved in a dialogue, the seller is really directing a tactical conversation as there is specific information he/she needs to build a sale."[10]

In some of the upcoming chapters, you will notice examples of storytelling that are presented as part of the tactical conversation that the seller uses in the dialogue of The 8 Step Upselling Advantage Script examples and again in the Script Analysis and Formula Breakdown explanations.

Strategy Two.
Persuasive Speaking.

The second strategy incorporates a persuasion technique to help you strengthen the eight step upselling advantage.

In 1963, two sociologists, named Paul Deutschberger and Eugene Weinstein, created Altercasting.

In short, altercasting is a theory that relies on the concept of persuasion, and it works like this. The goal of altercasting is to project an identity on your audience that is congruent with one's own goals, meaning the goal of your audience.[23]

"You can think of altercasting as cultivating the ground before you plant, says Robert Cialdini, a social psychologist and professor emeritus of psychology and marketing at Arizona State University, "Expert gardeners know that it doesn't matter how good the seed is unless you've prepared the soil to receive it optimally," he says.[24]

According to *The Wall Street Journal*, "There haven't been many research studies done on it since then, in part because it's labor-intensive to replicate in a lab, subject by subject. Psychologists say it's widely used in the real world—by advertisers, fundraisers, parents, teachers, spouses, and therapists, among others." [24]

In chapter one- how to be great at sales, you learned in lesson three that you need to learn how to prepare the sale to the customer; specifically, Howard Litwak taught us, *"the seller is really directing a tactical conversation as there is specific information he/she needs to build a sale."*[10]

When you incorporate altercasting in the eight step upselling advantage, essentially, you are casting the prospect into a role that he or she wants to be in.

Prior to approaching the prospect and beginning the eight step upselling advantage, "Ask yourself what role is central to his or her value system," says Frank Boster, a professor of communication at Michigan State University.[24]

If you are showing that you see your prospect in the way they want to be seen and that is positive, this can help you improve the tactical conversation to build the sale.

This is how altercasting is so effective in advertising, as it "is a strategy... for persuading people by forcing them in a social role, so that they will be inclined to behave according to that role." [23]

In chapter six, you will be able to see altercasting being used as part of the eight step upselling advantage, including when to use it and how it helps support and direct the sales conversation.

Strategy Three.
Follow a Script.

The third strategy that helps you understand how the eight step upselling advantage works is simply using a script. When you use a script, this can have the following effects on your sales conversation. It will help you build confidence. It can decrease stress for you. It will improve your voice tone. A script will also build comfort for you, allowing you to focus more on the sale instead of worrying about what to say next. In short, a script gives you a cheat sheet to work off of.

When you have a script that consists of the five lessons learned in chapter one, plus storytelling and some altercasting, these can all be effective techniques to help you succeed at utilizing the techniques taught in the eight step upselling advantage. In the next chapter, chapter three, you're going to see examples of a script for the eight step upselling advantage, and a little while later, in chapter six, you're going to see these strategies from chapter three again, as they are all used together in a larger, more complex eight step upselling advantage script.

Chapter 3

HOW TO UPSELL
with The 8 Step Upselling Advantage

In this chapter, you're going to learn the eight step upselling advantage, a specific systematic formula to upsell. This chapter will also explain to you the main objectives and goals for each step in The 8 Step Upselling Advantage. After these explanations, you will learn suggestions to help you easily memorize and remember the eight steps in the correct order.

By the end of this book, you will have word for word examples to learn from that were tested in live everyday sales scenarios. These examples were successful not only in increasing business sales, but were also instrumental in increasing employee efficiency. Remember from chapter one, we still want to increase your efficiency as a server, so we can help combat critiques such as "service that was lacking" and "inattentive waiters."

Most importantly though, the goal here is to teach you well enough so that, with enough practice, you will automatically be upselling naturally based on the formulas and examples that we are going to cover. Now, let's start explaining the upselling formula.

The Eight Step Upselling Advantage contains eight steps, presented on the next page in their order of steps 1-8, followed by an explanation of the individual goal that each step seeks to accomplish.

THE 8 STEP UPSELLING ADVANTAGE

1. ATTENTION PLEASE
2. BE INTERESTING
3. CREATE ASSURANCE
4. DESCRIBE
5. AWAKE DESIRE
6. BEAT THEIR TEST
7. CALL TO ACTION
8. DECISION TIME

THE 8 STEP UPSELLING ADVANTAGE EXPLAINED

Step 1- ATTENTION PLEASE- the main objective of this step is to attract your audience's curiosity, so they will listen to you.

Step 2- BE INTERESTING- the main objective of this step is to cultivate your audience's interest, so they can begin to understand how the new information they are about to learn is important to them and relates to their current situation.

Step 3- CREATE ASSURANCE- the main objective of this step is to promise that your offer will serve the reader well in certain ways that are appealing and beneficial to him or her.

Step 4- DESCRIBE- the main objective of this step is to tell them a short subtle story containing an attractive description of what you are selling.

Step 5- AWAKE DESIRE- the main objective of this step is to have your audience start desiring the need to take advantage of the benefits you offered in steps 2 and 3.

Step 6- BEAT THEIR TEST- the main objective of this step is to give examples of the product or service in use. This proves that the product or service has utility and worth and that he or she is going to want to take advantage of said worth.

Step 7- CALL TO ACTION- the main objective of this step is to urge the reader to take advantage of the promised values.

Step 8- DECISION TIME- the main objective of this step is to obtain a decision based on confidence in what you have said in steps two through seven about your product and service offered.

If you are wondering how to remember all eight steps in the correct order, here is a simple trick you can use to remember them.All you need to do is remember the following letters in this order, "A-B-C-D-A-B-C-D."

The first letter is "A" for Attention please. The Second letter is "B" for Be interesting. The third letter is another "C" for Create assurance. The fourth letter is "D" for Describe. The fifth letter is "A" for Awake desire. The sixth letter is another "B" for Beat their test. The seventh letter is another "C" for Call To Action. The eighth and last letter is "D" for Decision time.

Another way to help you learn and memorize the 8 step upselling advantage formula is to compose your own sentence based on the first letters of each step. A third way to help you memorize the eight step upselling advantage is to use the supplemental eight step upselling advantage workbook to develop your own customized script using examples and stories from your life. After you come up with your own customized script, you can then print out the worksheets to use as a cheat sheet, helping you learn the eight step upselling advantage faster.

In the next chapter, we will begin by introducing a script of how a phone call to order might go. Afterwards, we'll breakdown the phone conversation and dissect the 8 step upselling advantage formula. This will explain and help you and your employees understand how it works. Before we begin that, though, again, I want to let you know that using this formula and building employee skill level will take practice and effort. The nice part about using the formula, especially over the phone, is that your employee can read from a script right in front of them and the customer will never know. Afterwards, once your employee gets comfortable using the formula above as a guide, then he or she will begin to speak in their natural voice. The 8 step upselling advantage formula will become second nature to them when selling, and your time and efforts will have been time well spent. To get to this stage, though, we still have a little more ground to cover. The next chapter will help get us closer to this stage as we begin teaching the 8 step upselling advantage formula, scripts, and the formula breakdown.

Chapter 4

The 8 Step Upselling Advantage
Scripts, and Formula Explanation

THE 8 STEP UPSELLING ADVANTAGE FORMULA
PHONE CALL TO ORDER SCRIPT EXAMPLE

(Phone rings)

(Employee Answers)

Employee:	"Peyton and Lilly's Pizza. This is Peyton. How can I help you?"
Customer:	"Hi. I'd like to order a Large Pepperoni Pizza and one dozen medium wings please."
Employee:	"Ok. Can I get your phone number please?
Customer:	"725-3231"
Employee:	"Got it. Thanks. Will this be a pick up or delivery?"
Customer:	"Pick up."
Employee:	"Ok. Thanks. Next, can I get your name please?"
Customer:	"Marley."

Employee: "Marley. OK. Hey Marley, I don't know if you'd be interested in saving some money tonight, or if you've heard but we now have Garlic Knots. They're delicious. You get 12 of them in an order. They're homemade right here in our shop, made with our signature dough and perfect mix of garlic and butter, and they're delicious. I've tried them myself, and in fact my friend Mike has been ordering them with his pizza and wings. He says they're great plain and even better when you dip them into wing sauce. Would you like to try them today while they're on sale? Normally the cost is $4.95, but because we just started offering them, they're only $3.99. Would you like to try them while they're on sale to see if you like them?

(Pause. Don't say anything at all now. Let the customer be the next to speak).

Customer: "Yeah that sounds good. What would that bring my total to, the pizza, wings and garlic knots?"

Employee: "Let's see you're picking up the pizza so you get a discount there, the wings are only $6.99, if you add in the garlic knots on sale with tax and everything your total would only be $21.78."

Customer: "Ok I'll take it."

Employee: "Great. Thanks. Just to make sure you're getting the Large Pepperoni, one dozen medium, and an order of garlic knots?"

Customer: "Yup. That's correct."

Employee: "Thanks. You can stop by in 30 minutes to pick it up."

Customer: "Ok Thanks. See ya then."

End Phone Script Example

THE 8 STEP UPSELLING ADVANTAGE FORMULA
PHONE CALL TO ORDER SCRIPT ANALYSIS

Summary of The Sale: This is a good example of The 8 Step Upselling Advantage being utilized correctly and effectively. The phone call to order script example contains what occurs when a customer places an order. You probably noticed a majority of it is a standard call to order, with the exception of the interaction when the employee begins to say "Marley. OK. Hey Marley ..." This paragraph is where the employee is using the eight step upselling advantage formula. On the next page, I've copied the paragraph alone, so you can read it again. Afterwards, I've included a breakdown of when the individual steps in the eight step upselling advantage formula actually occur.

Employee:	"Marley. OK. Hey Marley, I don't know if you'd be interested in saving some money tonight, or if you've heard but we now have Garlic Knots. They're delicious. You get 12 of them in an order. They're homemade right here in our shop, made with our signature dough and perfect mix of garlic and butter, and they're delicious. I've tried them myself, and in fact my friend Mike has been ordering them with his pizza and wings. He says they're great plain and even better when you dip them into wing sauce. Would you like to try them today while they're on sale? Normally, the cost is $4.95, but because we just started offering them, they're only $3.99. Would you like to try them while they're on sale to see if you like them?

**THE 8 STEP UPSELLING ADVANTAGE FORMULA
BREAKDOWN in PHONE SCRIPT EXAMPLE #1**

Step 1- ATTENTION PLEASE- This step occurs very quickly and simply when Peyton says, "Hey Marley." Remember the main objective of this step is to attract your audience's curiosity, so they will listen to you. Immediately after saying "Hey Marley," Peyton goes right into step 2, which is described next.

Step 2- BE INTERESTING- This step occurs immediately after getting attention. To provoke interest, Peyton says, "I don't know if you'd be interested in saving some money tonight, or if you've heard but we now have Garlic Knots." Remember, the main objective of this step is to cultivate your audience's interest, so they can begin to understand how the new information they are about to learn is important to them and relates to their current situation.

Step 3- CREATE ASSURANCE- "They're delicious." Depending on your product, this step can be short or long. It doesn't really matter, because in step 4, you'll actually continue step 3. This will make more sense when you read step 4 next. Remember, the main objective of this step is to make a promise that your offer will serve the customer well in certain ways that are appealing and beneficial to him or her.

Step 4- DESCRIBE- The main objective of this step is to tell them a short subtle story containing an attractive description of what you are selling. In phone script example #1, this happens immediately after step 3. The picture is painted when Peyton starts to describe the Garlic Knots by saying, "They're homemade right here in our shop, made with our signature dough and perfect mix of garlic and butter..."

Step 5- AWAKE DESIRE- "They're homemade right here in our shop, made with our signature dough and perfect mix of garlic and butter..." In phone script example one, steps three, four, and five are all working together in the same sentence. By painting the picture of the garlic knots being homemade right here in the shop, and how the customer gets 12 in their order, Peyton is also rousing desire. Depending on your product, this step can be short or long. Remember, the main objective of this step is to have your audience start desiring the need to take advantage of the benefits you have offered in steps two and three.

Step 6- BEAT THEIR TEST- "I've tried them myself, and in fact my friend Mike has been ordering them with his pizza and wings. He says they're great plain and even better when you dip them into wing sauce." Here, the employee is proving the promise that they just made in step three. Not only does Peyton accomplish this by stating that the garlic knots are delicious, but she also states that her friend has ordered them also. Peyton then subtly uses steps three, four, and five again (create assurance, describe, and awake desire), when she says that, according to Mike, the garlic knots are great plain and even better when you dip them into wing sauce. Remember, the main objective of this step is to give examples of the product or service in use. This proves that the product or service has utility and worth and that he or she is going to want to take advantage of said worth. In phone script example #1, Peyton is specifically stating how great Mike says the garlic knots taste when dipped into wing sauce. This is a great example, because what a coincidence, the customer ordered a dozen wings in that order also.

Step 7- CALL TO ACTION- Step seven is simply your call to action. This is where you try to get the customer to commit to buying the product. In phone script example #1, this occurs when Peyton says, "Would you like to try them today while they're on sale? They're delicious. You get 12 of them in an order. Normally, the cost is $4.95, but because we just started offering them, they're only $3.99." It is important to note also that, immediately after Peyton asks the customer if they would like to try them today while they are on sale, she very quickly restates the benefits of how many the customer gets and the price in one last effort to rouse desire before the customer makes their final decision. Remember, the main objective of this step is to urge the reader to take advantage of the promised values.

Step 8- DECISION TIME- Finally, in step eight, Peyton asks one last time, "Would you like to try them while they're on sale to see if you like them?" (Pause. Don't say anything at all now. Let them be the next to speak). Note the pause. The best thing to say after giving your sales pitch is nothing at all. Let the customer be the next to speak. This will force them into making the decision. This will also keep the employee from talking too much. Remember, the main objective of this step is to obtain a decision based on confidence in what you have said in steps two through seven about your product and service offered.

In the next chapter, we are going to cover some scenarios and questions that might occur while you are learning The 8 Step Upselling Advantage. These scenarios and questions are based on the phone script example you just read in chapter 4. After each question and scenario presented, you will then read some suggestions and advice on how to handle these situations.

Chapter 5

PHONE SCRIPT EXAMPLE
Troubleshooting Guide

While the number of questions and possibilities are too numerous to cover in this section alone, I am going to try to answer as many of the most frequent contingencies here to try to help you understand why I said what I said when I said it.

Q: Why did I use the eight step upselling advantage formula later in the order taking sequence as opposed to starting the conversation with it?

A: I did this because I (or Peyton the employee) wanted to see what the customer wanted to order first. This has two main advantages, the first one being that I wanted to see what he wanted to order before I tried to sell him something additional. Once I found out what he wanted to order, I then used   this information to help me sell him the new product. This is exactly what I did in phone script example #1. Peyton told the customer how Mike said the Garlic Knots taste great when he dips them into his wing sauce. The customer was already ordering wings, which I learned by letting the customer place the order first. The Garlic Knots just happened to be what I had been selling well all night that night, so why change what works (more on this later)? In Phone Script example #1, instead of Garlic Knots, I easily could've tried to upsell a soda to go along with the pizza instead. The concept is the same. If I didn't let the customer place the order first and learn that he only wanted to order pizza and wings, I wouldn't have known to sell the soda after. The second advantage is that I wanted to let the customer think he was in charge of the order and this was just a normal order. I didn't want to try to sell him something immediately, because it would've been too easy for him to say "No" right from the start. This also could have potentially put the customer's guard up, meaning when they say "No" once, it is a little harder to get them to say "Yes" afterwards.

Q: What if the customer did say "No" in the middle of the script? What do you do then?

A: By choosing the words I used in phone script example #1, this situation was unlikely to occur. I selected these words and presented them when I did specifically for a reason. The reason I phrased step two (be interesting) using, "I don't know if you'd be interested in saving some money tonight, or if you've heard but we now have Garlic Knots", is because it would've been socially awkward for the customer to interrupt me to say, "No I'm not interested in saving money." Also, after I mentioned garlic knots, this allowed me immediately to go into step three (create assurance) and continue on with the entire 8 step formula. Again, the customer usually won't interrupt. Finally, two things will happen once you've completed step eight (decision time). The customer will either say, "Yes" or "No Thanks." If they say "Yes", congratulations, but if they say "No", don't get discouraged. You've just gotten good experience and built your comfort level some more. Besides, when the customer says "No", it doesn't mean you did a bad job. There are too many unknown variables that you have no control over, meaning for all you know, the customer might be on a budget and can't afford anything more than they already ordered that night. In this case, simply say, "Ok, that's fine I just wanted to let you know about them. You should definitely try them next time though." That would complete the order.

Q: What if I mess up step 2 and accidently first ask the customer, "Would you like to try our new Garlic Knots tonight?"

A: Ok. If you accidently ask the customer if they want to try the new product first, you've presented step 8 (decision time) first instead of be interesting (step 2) first. Two things can happen in this scenario. If they say "Yes", congratulations. You don't have to do any more work. If they say "No", ignore the answer and immediately start talking about step 3 (create assurance) and don't stop talking until you present step 8 again (decision time). "They're delicious. They're homemade right here in our shop. You get 12 of them in an order, and they're delicious. I've tried them myself, and in fact my friend Mike has been ordering them with his pizza and wings. He says they're great plain and even better when you dip them into wing sauce. Would you like to try them today while they're on sale? They're delicious. You get 12 of them in an order, normally the cost is $4.95, but because we just started offering them, they're only $3.99. Would you like to try them while they're on sale to see if you like them?" Again, this is very important. Don't stop talking. The reason being is that, after you present step 8 the second time (obtain decision), this time after going through steps 3-8, you can only get one of two possible answers. The first is "No" again. If they say no again, politely say, "Ok, I just wanted to let you know about them" and carry on with the order. You've at least done the best you can. If they say "Yes", they don't say   just "Yes." The reply usually is more like, "Ok yeah you talked me into it" or "Yeah that sounds good actually." Congratulations, you recovered nicely and still made the sale.

Q: What is the easiest and fastest way to learn the eight step upselling advantage formula?

A: The easiest and fastest way to learn the eight step upselling advantage formula is to do the following:

1.   Pick one item and focus on selling just that item the entire night. This will get you used to becoming more comfortable and concentrating on the formula rather than what to say next. In short, there is less confusion this way when you are practicing the same script 20 times a night as opposed to practicing 20 different scripts that each sell a different item just one time a night. In short, why change what works?

2.   Have a cheat sheet prepared. If you're on the phone, have the sheet of what you're going to say in front of you. If you're taking the order in person, have the cheat sheet on your computer or have notes on your pad of paper. No one is going to suspect you of using a cheat sheet, and honestly, who cares if they do?

3.   Develop your own style. Don't be afraid to let your personality show. This will keep you more at ease and will make the process more fun and enjoyable. Steps 1-8 do not

have to happen one right after the other immediately. For example, try incorporating something in common that you might have with your audience. What I mean by that is this: let's say a customer has come in to place an order in person and you see that they're wearing a NY baseball shirt. When you get to step 6 (beat their test), instead of saying "...and in fact my friend Mike has been ordering them..." I would've said "...in fact my friend Kolin, who actually I just went to their stadium with, I like your shirt by the way, anyways Kolin has been ordering them..." This is going to make the sale feel more natural and like a conversation to you, and this allows the opportunity to have a conversation afterwards, which will leave the customer satisfied with the customer service. They're going to feel like, instead of ordering from a restaurant, they were supporting friends. Loyalty has its value; just make sure your product presentation is as great as your customer service skills.

4. Last, answer the phone or take as many orders as possible and practice your script for the night when you do. Remember this skill needs developing. The more practice and effort that is devoted, the better you are going to get.

Q: What do you advise if this is still too hard for employees to understand or if an employee wants to start with something easier to build their comfort level?

A: Two examples and scripts below both illustrate a good introduction for beginning upselling and getting the employee comfortable:

The first example is this:

> After the initial order has taken place but prior to the employee asking if the customer "would like anything else", encourage the employee to keep the sale going by asking the customer something simple such as:

> 1.   "Do you need any soda to go with that?" (An alternate question in place of step 1 would be, "You look thirsty. Do you want some soda with your order tonight?"

> 2.   If they say "Yes", ask them, "What kind and size." If they say "No", then politely say, "Ok. That's fine. You looked thirsty, so I just wanted to see if you needed something to drink to go with your order."

> 3.   If the answer is "Yes", instead of asking "how many?" ask if they'd like "12" or something totally obscure. It's important to say this with a smile on your face, nonchalantly or casually.

> 4.   The customer responds usually with a smile and a laugh then replies, "No Thanks. Just one please."

> 5.   Another similar technique is, whenever a customer orders a pizza, DO NOT have the employee ask, "What kind of toppings do you want on it?" Instead, have the

employee say, "Would you like anchovies on that?" and then smile.

Both of these responses usually produce smiles on customers' faces, and the spontaneity of the conversation often gets the customer laughing from enjoyment. These are key factors, as the combination of smiling and enjoying what should have been a simple generic phone call now has the customer associating your restaurant with appreciation and remembering how personable the staff is. Not only will they think of you next time they are hungry, but we are helping to develop the employee's customer service skills. This is important in many ways, not only in terms of customer satisfaction and exceptional customer service skills, but you and your colleagues can take this small foundation and build on your newly acquired skills, eventually all the way up to learning the eight step upselling advantage formula. The primary objective completed and emphasized here is that, once you get comfortable taking orders on the phone and learn how much "fun" it is to answer the phone, you'll soon begin to think of other ways to increase sales.

The second example illustrates a good introduction for beginning upselling and getting you comfortable through assigning tasks. Based on your individual skill levels, try concentrating on selling an extra soda to each customer, or you could concentrate on specific side items on the menu to complement customers' orders. A third option for you is to focus on selling items made at certain stations inside the shop. The third option works especially well on a Friday night, when your Boss's husband is at the shop helping on the fryer station. Personally, whenever I had this opportunity, at every chance available, I tried to sell as many chicken wings as possible.

Putting the two examples mentioned above into practice, eventually you will not only be comfortable and proficient at answering the phone and taking orders, but you'll also begin to see how easy and fun it can be to get a customer to spend $25.00 when initially they were only planning on getting a $15.00 pizza.

When beginning to train yourself on the eight step upselling advantage, one way to relate to the new lessons is to learn the new material by relating it to something you are already familiar with. By using the examples above, you will learn customer service skills, while increasing your comfort and skill set levels. The entire time you're doing all this, you're continuing to re-emphasize what you learned when you started reading chapter one lesson one on how to make money...

> *"The only way to earn money is by providing people with services or products which are needed and useful."* [7]

In the next chapter, we are going to be reading about a fictional character named Bill, who started working at a restaurant in Albany, NY. While Bill was working there, he learned about the eight step upselling advantage and practiced the techniques and strategies he read in this book. A few years later, Bill graduated from college, and he used his new sales skill set in his new career.

Chapter 6

HOW TO USE
The 8 Step Upselling Advantage
when you get a new job or in your career

Now that you have learned The 8 Step Upselling Advantage, how it works, the complete formula, and a breakdown of the strategy showing how each step works in conjunction with the entire method, chapter six is going to teach you how you can utilize The 8 Step Upselling Advantage in a new job or career outside the restaurant industry. To begin this journey, we're going to take you first to the capital of New York State.

In September 2011, Kevin Everleth opened a restaurant on the edge of the Pine Hills neighborhood, called the Capital City Gastropub located at 261 New Scotland Avenue in Albany, NY. Shortly afterwards, Everleth brought on Adam Baker as the general manager of the Capital City Gastropub. In May 2013, Baker and his business partner, Daniel Silver, bought the restaurant from Everleth and Adam, and Dan became the new owners of the Capital City Gastropub.[25]

Today, the Capital City Gastropub is known as one of the five best burger places in the capital region. The restaurant also offers a large selection of craft beers made by some of the world's most renowned breweries, which are presented in a unique and comfortable environment.[26, 27, 28]

In addition to being known as one of the best burger places in the capital region, The Capital City Gastropub is also known as one of the best brunch spots in Albany.[29]

Recently, a 21-year-old waiter, named Bill, began working at the Capital City Gastropub to help save money for college while he was on summer vacation.

One day, Bill showed up to work the Sunday brunch shift, and he learned from Dan and Adam that the restaurant is now going to be offering a new item on a trial basis to see how well the product sells and how well it is received by the customers. This new change was made as part of Adam and Dan's efforts to improve the quality of their menu and the restaurant service to their customers. Dan informed Bill that Capital City Gastropub is now serving Devil Daves Bloody Marys. Adam also shares some of the specifics of the new product, so Bill has material to work with as he composes his upselling script for Devil Daves during the brunch shift that day.

Devil Daves Bloody Mary Sticks were officially launched in May 2018 by Ryan Pakenas, a talented sous chef, bartender, and e-commerce entrepreneur.[30, 31] They are the world's first instant Bloody Mary stick pack, and they are exploding in the B2B market. The product is especially popular in the Restaurant and Airline Industries, thanks to it being a non-perishable solution that solves everyday problems, such as spoilage, expensive cost, and weak taste that often are challenges with making Bloody Marys.[32, 33]

Devil Daves Bloody Marys spice mix contains horseradish, dried vegan Worcestershire, celery salt, cracked black pepper, garlic, onion and more to create a taste just like the real thing because it is the real thing. All of the ingredients are vegan free, gluten free, and non GMO, consisting of everything you would put in a Bloody Mary to give the beverage a classic taste that is also a huge hit with consumers in the B2C market. Devil Daves Bloody Marys are also available to purchase online at devildaves.com and on Amazon Prime.[30, 31, 34, 35, 36]

Now given all this information mentioned about the sales formula, the restaurant, and the new product, let's look at how Bill utilizes The 8 Step Upselling Advantage to try to increase sales of Devil Daves Bloody Marys and sales for the Capital City Gastropub during his Sunday brunch shift.

THE 8 STEP UPSELLING ADVANTAGE FORMULA
DEVIL DAVES BLOODY MARY SCRIPT

Employee: "Good morning. My name is Bill."

Customer: "Morning."

Employee: "I'll be your server today. Right now, we are featuring a drink special called Devil Daves Bloody Mary, and it is an absolute hit. It consists of Tomato Juice, vodka, along with the right blend of dry spices to give it a solid classic Bloody Mary taste. It is Vegan and Gluten Free and kind of a new item in the restaurant, so you get to be one of the first to try it, but I do know that Devil Daves Bloody Marys are a huge hit online- nothing but 5 star ratings on both Amazon and Google. Would you like to try one?"

(Pause. Bill lets the customer be the next to speak).

Customer: "That sounds amazing, but I have to pass. I don't like Tomato juice at all."

Employee: "OK. That's fine and totally

understandable. Would you like a water or

juice instead?"

THE 8 STEP UPSELLING ADVANTAGE FORMULA
DEVIL DAVES BLOODY MARY SCRIPT ANALYSIS

Summary of The Sale: Even though Bill did not get a sale here, this is still an excellent script that utilized The 8 Step Upselling Advantage. In chapter 5, we discussed, sometimes there are unknown variables that prevent a sale. In the Devil Daves Bloody Mary upsell script example, unfortunately, the customer simply doesn't like tomato juice. However, this was good practice and warm up for Bill because, in this scenario, Bill will have another opportunity to upsell the customer when the customer orders his meal and possibly even a third opportunity offering coffee or dessert after the meal. Next, let's check out the upselling formula breakdown and script analysis.

Step 1- ATTENTION PLEASE- This step occurs very quickly and simply when Bill says, "Good morning. My name is Bill." Remember, the main objective of this step is to capture your audience's attention, so they will listen to you. Immediately after saying "Good morning..." Bill goes right into step 2, which is described next.

Step 2- BE INTERESTING- This step occurs immediately after getting attention. To provoke interest, Bill says, ""I'll be your server today. Right now, we are featuring a drink special called Devil Daves Bloody Mary..." Remember, the main objective of this step is to cultivate your audience's interest, so they can begin to understand how the new information they are about to learn is important to them and relates to their current situation.

Step 3- CREATE ASSURANCE- "...and it is an absolute hit." Depending on your product, this step can be short or long. It doesn't really matter, because in step 4, you'll actually continue step 3. This is will make more sense when you read step 4 next. Remember, the main objective of this step is to create assurance that your offer will serve the customer well in certain ways that are appealing and beneficial to him or her.

Step 4- DESCRIBE- The main objective of this step is to tell them a short subtle story containing an attractive description of what you are selling. In the Devil Daves example, this happens immediately after step 3. Here is when Bill starts to describe the Bloody Mary by saying, "It consists of Tomato Juice, vodka, along with the right blend of dry spices to give it a solid classic Bloody Mary taste. It is Vegan and Gluten Free and kind of a new item in the restaurant, so you get to be one of the first to try it..."

Step 5- AWAKE DESIRE- "...It consists of Tomato Juice, vodka, along with the right blend of dry spices to give it a solid classic Bloody Mary taste. It is Vegan and Gluten Free and kind of a new item in the restaurant, so you get to be one of the first to try it..." In the Devil Daves upselling example, steps three, four, and five are all working together in the same sentence by describing in detail the beverage. How it contains tomato juice, vodka, the right blend of spices to give it a solid classic Bloody Mary taste, and then adding the additional benefits that the Bloody Mary is Vegan free and Gluten free, and that the customer gets to get special treatment by becoming one of the first people to taste a Devil Daves Bloody Mary... all of this combined helps Bill try to awake and even create a desire for the special   beverage. Again, depending on your product, this step can be short or long. Remember, the main objective of this step is to have your audience start desiring the need to take advantage of the benefits you offered in steps two and three.

Step 6- BEAT THEIR TEST- "...but I do know that Devil Daves Bloody Marys are a huge hit online- nothing but 5 star ratings on both Amazon and Google..." Here Bill is proving the promise that he just made in steps three, four and five. Not only does Bill accomplish this by stating that Devil Daves Bloody Marys are a huge hit online, but he also specifically states that the beverage choice has received nothing but 5 star ratings on both amazon and google. Remember, the main objective of this step is to give examples of the product or service in use. This proves that the product or service has utility and worth and that he or she is going to want to take advantage of said worth. In the Devil Daves upselling example, Bill is specifically mentioning the 5 star review to attempt to remove any skepticism, beating any doubt that the customer might have regarding if he or she should try the product.

Step 7- CALL TO ACTION- Step seven is simply your call to action. This is where you try to get the customer to commit to buying the product. In the Devil Daves upsell example, step 7 occurs when Bill says, "...would you like to try one?"

Step 8- DECISION TIME- Finally, after Bill asks, "...would you like to try one?" step 7 then segues into step 8 (decision time). Bill actually doesn't need to say anything when he reaches step 8. In the Devil Daves Bloody Mary upsell example, step 8 (decision time) happens simply when Bill pauses and lets the customer be the next to speak. The pause is his opportunity to acquire the decision. It is not necessary here to repeat the question if the customer would like to try one. Remember, the main objective of this step is to obtain a decision based on confidence in what you have said in steps two through seven about your product and service offered.

Fast forward three years. Bill has now graduated from college with a Bachelor's Degree in Music Industry. Recognizing his passion for music combined with the increase in Sales Engineer job opportunities, Bill has accepted a Sales Engineer position at a well-known music gear corporation in his home state. Here at his new position, Bill finds himself answering questions, giving music advice, and educating customers. Bill helps customers discover that the sound they're looking for and the gear they need can be found through products the corporation has available for purchase. The catch here is that the music gear corporation is all online only. Bill does not see his customers. Bill sells music gear based on people finding the products online. If they are hesitant about purchasing after finding the music gear on the corporation's website or if they have questions before purchasing, they can then call Bill.

As a sales engineer, Bill quickly realizes that, by combining his knowledge in the music industry with the upselling skills he learned from reading The 8 Step Upselling Advantage book and then practicing The 8 Step Upselling Advantage while he was working as a waiter at the Capital City Gastropub, Bill can now use his upselling skills and experience in his new sales engineer position. Let's check out a possible phone call that Bill might experience and how he utilizes the 8 step upselling advantage in this scenario to drive sales.

THE 8 STEP UPSELLING ADVANTAGE FORMULA
MUSIC GEAR SALES ENGINEER SCRIPT

Employee: "Good afternoon! This is your sale engineer Bill speaking. How can I help you?"

Customer: "Bill! What's up, dude? This is Elvis calling."

Employee: "Elvis! What's going on, dude? How are you? Is this your first time calling the music gear corporation? How'd you hear about us?"

Customer: "Yeah man, this is my first time calling you guys. I found you while I was searching on the internet for a new Bass Guitar."

Employee: "OK that's cool. Are you a Bass Player? What are your primary and secondary instruments? Also, what are you hoping to accomplish with the new Bass?"

Customer: "No, I'm not really a Bass Player. I'm a singer, but I also play piano, and I have some guitars. My mother, Abbey, her birthday is coming up soon, and I want to record a song that I wrote for her and also sing another one of her favorites for her too then put them on a record for her birthday present this year. I'm playing all of the instruments on the tracks myself, plus I'm singing, and I don't want to sound like a barking dog when I go in there to record so I figured I should start to practice all of my parts now, so I know them solid before I go into the studio to record these songs. I need a Bass, so I can practice the Bass parts before I go into the studio to lay down the tracks. I was looking at possibly picking up either an Ivan Terrible Thor SS Bass or maybe the Thunder N' Lightning Bird Bass. Are you familiar with those two at all? What do you think of them?"

Employee: "OK cool, cool I got you. I am definitely familiar with both of those Basses. I don't own them, but I have played them both before. Your situation is one that I can definitely help you out with, dude, as I also play Bass. I have some follow up questions though. What bass sound are you looking for the tracks to have? Also, are you a teenager? Younger than that? Adult? You don't sound like a kid, but I just want to make sure first."

Customer: "OK Awesome. Yeah man. I'm in college. 20 years old. The Bass sound I'm looking for is similar to that old Motown sound."

Employee: "OK that's cool. Perfect. Here are my thoughts and advice on everything that you just mentioned based on my skills and experience. The Ivan Terrible Thor SS Bass is an alright Bass, especially at a price of $175.95; however, this Bass is kind of small as it is meant more for a younger musician. I think if you were to purchase this Bass, the compact size would make it more difficult for you to play being that it will probably be uncomfortable. I've tried playing one before, and while it is a good beginner Bass for a younger musician, the size limits its capabilities. For example, it is harder to play slap on it given the compact size and location of the pickups on the body. As far as the Thunder N' Lightning Bird Bass. This Bass rocks! I absolutely love it. It is comfortable, looks cool, and sounds good. The reason that I do not own it is because it produces a very specific tone that I don't really need. Also, while the description of the instrument states that it is made of a maple neck, if you look at picture three on the website, you will notice that the maple neck is stained so it closely matches the color of the rosewood fingerboard. While this looks great in appearance, given your situation of trying to learn songs quickly, I think that this Bass will take you longer to become comfortable and adjusted to fretting the notes as accurately and quickly as possible based on the design of the neck. Also, this Bass is not really known for that old Motown sound that you are going for. With all of that being said, I would like to suggest and ask you to take a look at the Bass called the Standard Precise. This was the Bass that was used on the old Motown tunes, and it will give you the sound that you're looking for.

Customer: "Hang on, searching for Standard Precise now. OK found it!"

Employee: "Good. Now I know that you're seeing that the cost is $624.99, which may seem out of your budget, but this will actually work to your advantage- here is how; right now the cost of the Thunder N Lightning Bird is $349.99 and when you add tax you were probably planning on spending close to $400 even with the free shipping. I can save you over $300 in your pocket today if you wanted to take advantage of this opportunity. Right now we are offering a limited time special finance offer on the Standard Precise Bass where if you purchase this Bass in any one of the five color options then you can pay off the Bass within 36 months including 0% interest. So while the Standard Precise Bass might cost more at $624.99, if you decide to take advantage of the special finance promotion that we have going on right now, you can actually get that Bass for 36 monthly payments of only $17.36 per month. So instead of spending close to $400 on the other Bass that you were thinking about, you could actually get the Standard Precise this week with our free expedited shipping included, and it would only cost you $17.36 today. Saving you over $300 which is huge because studio time is expensive and that $300 savings is more money that you could put towards the budget of recording the songs for your mom. There is a catch though that I want to warn you about. The special finance promotion ends in two days. This opportunity is not available everyday it is a limited time offer. I really think this is a great deal for you though as you will be saving a ton of money, and this Bass will give you the sound that you're looking for. Plus, it's comfortable, looks beautiful and it is well known in the industry giving it a higher resale value if you ever decide to sell it or trade it in in the future for different gear. And last, dude, if you get the Bass and find that it is really not the instrument for you, you are able to return the Bass to us for a refund or store credit if you want. It's a very simple process, but based on what you told me, I really believe you're going to like this Bass and it is the right one for you. Would you like to purchase the Standard Precise Bass for only 36 monthly payments of $17.36?

(Pause. Bill lets the customer be the next to speak).

Customer: Holy smokes! Absolutely I want that deal. This sounds great, man!

Employee: Yeah dude, it really is a super deal. You made the right call and really lucked out with the timing to pick up this Bass now. I just have a couple of more questions. We also have cases for the Standard Precise Bass. I wanted to mention this as you sound like a talented musician and talented musicians are usually very smart and they also are very protective of their instruments. A case would definitely help you protect your Bass when you are traveling back and forth to the studio, and if you ever decided to resell in the future, you'll be protecting your investment by purchasing a case. Cases for the Standard Precise Bass only cost $99.99 and you can finance that along with the Bass as a package so if you added on the case, instead of $17.36, the new monthly payment would only be $20.14 for 36 months. It is only an extra $2.78 a month. To me, this is a no brainer to help protect your investment and another excellent deal for you. Do you want to purchase the case also?

(Pause. Bill lets the customer be the next to speak).

Customer: "Good thinking. Yes, I'll add on the case also."

Employee: "Smart move dude. I would've done the same thing if I were in your shoes. OK so that was question one; the second question that I wanted to ask you was you said that you were going for the old Motown sound. The Standard Precise Bass comes stock with roundwound strings; however, I'm not sure how much you've read about on the classic Motown sound but the Bass players on those records all used flatwound strings on their Standard Precise Basses. I highly, highly recommend that you add flatwounds to your new Bass. They are more comfortable to play and give you that true sound that you're looking for so the songs will sound their absolute best for your mom. If you wanted to add a set, they are only $34.99 for a 4 string set but again if you purchase these today, we can add

them in on the finance package so if you

picked up the flatwound set also, your cost

would only increase by 97 cents a month to

just $21.11. That includes everything, dude,

the Standard Precise Bass, the new case,

and the new set of flatwound strings. I can

have all 3 of these items out to you and on

your doorstep in 2-3 days if you want to go

for the deal now. Plus, most importantly,

dude, it's for your Mom. Not only will she

think you sound great on the record but

you'll also have personal satisfaction of

success knowing you recorded the best

sound possible with this gear. That feeling

is totally worth it especially when you look

back and it only cost you an extra 97 cents

a month. Do you want to add the

flatwound strings also to your order?

(Pause. Bill lets the customer be the next to speak).

Customer: "Oh my goodness, you're exactly right. I almost forgot about the flatwound strings on the Motown Bass sound. Thanks for reminding me. Yes, absolutely I want them. Heavy gauge please."

Employee: "Cool, Cool. Sounds good, Elvis. I actually just have one more question that I just thought of... Jamerson used to play with a classic B-15 amp to get that old Motown sound..." [37]

Customer: "Hey Bill. Sorry, I don't mean to interrupt but just to let you know I'm actually good as far as an amp goes. The studio actually already has an amp available for me to use, and as far as practicing before then I was just going to plug the bass into my keyboard amp for now. "

Employee: "Haha. Awesome, man. OK cool, you've already thought of that then. Good glad to hear that that plan is going to work out for you. Alright Elvis, I think that you're all set, man. I am just going to repeat the total order quickly and ask you if you accept the order and give me permission to charge then I think we will have everything taken care of here. Just a quick recap, you are purchasing one Standard Precise Bass at $624.99, one Bass case at $99.99, and one Heavy gauge flatwound Bass strings set for $34.99. Bringing your total to $759.97 to be paid in 36 equal monthly payments of $21.11 each. Do you give me permission to charge your card to make this purchase for you?"

Customer: "Yes, all of that is correct. I give you permission."

Employee: "Hold up! Dude, I forgot to ask. What color Bass do you want? The color options are Black Diamond Rubble, Frog N' Foam Sophie Green, Chocolate Brown Lewis,

French Bulldog Bunny White, or Buffy Copper Penny."

Customer: "Good catch, Bill! The Bass has to be Black Diamond Rubble."

Employee: "OK cool, cool. Thanks for the info. Alright one second... and you're all set, man. The charge was approved. Elvis, thanks a ton for calling. It was great chatting with you and good luck on recording those songs. I am sure your mom will love her birthday present, dude!"

Customer: "Excellent! Thank you so much for the help, Bill!"

Employee: "No problem, man. Thanks for calling us. I'm going to email you a copy of the receipt. If there's anything else I can help you with, don't hesitate to call me back."

Customer: "Sounds great. Thanks again, man. Have a good one, Bill!"

Employee: "Have a good one, Elvis! Rock on, dude."

THE 8 STEP UPSELLING ADVANTAGE FORMULA MUSIC GEAR SALES ENGINEER SCRIPT ANALYSIS

Summary of The Sale: The music gear sales engineer script is an excellent example that displays everything taught so far being utilized effectively. Here, Bill was able to change a potential sale of $175.95 (if Elvis purchased the Terrible Thor), and what easily could had been a $349.99 sale (if Elvis had purchased the Thunder Bass). But, instead, through applying the techniques and strategies learned starting from chapter one in how to be great at sales all the way through using his skill set mastery of The 8 Step Upselling Advantage, Bill was able to turn this sales opportunity into a sales success story with the final purchase total being $759.97. Next, let's examine how this occurred as we thoroughly analyze the sales script.

THE 8 STEP UPSELLING ADVANTAGE FORMULA ANALYSIS PORTRAYING LESSONS FROM CHAPTERS 1-3

The Greeting

Employee: *"Good afternoon! This is your sales engineer*

Bill speaking. How can I help you?"

The Greeting used here is an excellent choice of words by Sales Engineer Bill. The first reason is because it begins Step 1 (Attention Please) of the 8 step upselling advantage. The second reason is because when Bill introduces himself as "This is your sales engineer Bill," he is demonstrating lesson three in how to be great at sales that you learned in chapter one. A quick recap for you; lesson three was "You need to learn how to prepare the sale to the customer." When Bill introduces himself as "This is your sales engineer Bill," he is establishing that this is a long-term relationship. Bill also sets himself up a contingency plan for future sales. If Elvis did not want to purchase on this call, then Bill has a plan already set in place, thanks to his greeting. Elvis can call Bill when timing is better to purchase the Bass or an even better option. Bill can follow up with Elvis in a few months to carry on the sales conversation, check in on how the recording went, and let Elvis know about an upcoming sale in case that he was still interested in picking up a new Bass.

Opportunity #1 for upsell– Bill sells Elvis a better Bass

> *Employee:*   *"Elvis! What's going on, dude? How are*
>
> *you? Is this your first time calling the*
>
> *music gear corporation? How'd you hear*
>
> *about us?"*

The reply above begins step 2 (be interesting) of the upselling formula. In this reply, when Bill asks, "Is this your first time calling the music gear corporation?" and "How'd you hear about us?" Bill is building on lesson three in how to be great at sales: "You need to learn how to prepare the sale to the customer." These questions demonstrate the advice from Howard Litwak that teaches, "Although the prospect should feel that they are involved in a dialogue, the seller is really directing a tactical conversation as there is specific information that he/she needs to build a sale."[17] Elvis then replies, and Bill continues to direct the tactical conversation...

> *Customer:*   *"Yeah man, this is my first time calling*
>
> *you guys. I found you while I was*

> *searching on the internet for a new Bass*
>
> *Guitar."*

Employee: *"OK that's cool. Are you a Bass Player?*

What are your primary and secondary

instruments? Also, what are you hoping to

accomplish with the new Bass?"

Here, when Bill asks Elvis, "Are you a Bass Player? What are your primary and secondary instruments? Also, what are you hoping to accomplish with the new Bass?" Bill is building on lesson three of how to be great at sales, and Bill efficiently begins to use his knowledge of lesson two of how to be great at sales: "You need to learn the most important secret of salesmanship." The most important secret of salesmanship was taught in chapter one when you heard the story of Clayton Hunsicker giving the following sales advice to Frank Bettger: "The most important secret of salesmanship is to find out what the other fellow wants, then help him find the best way to get it."[8] Next, let's read the answers that Elvis supplied Bill:

Customer: *"No, I'm not really a Bass Player. I'm a*

singer, but I also play piano, and I have

some guitars. My mother, Abbey, her

birthday is coming up soon and I want to

record a song that I wrote for her and also

sing another one of her favorites for her

too then put them on a record for her

birthday present this year. I'm playing all

of the instruments on the tracks myself,

plus I'm singing, and I don't want to

sound like a barking dog when I go in

there to record, so I figured I should start

to practice all of my parts now so I know

them solid before I go into the studio to

record these songs. I need a Bass, so I can

practice the Bass parts before I go into the

studio to lay down the tracks. I was

looking at possibly picking up either an

Ivan Terrible Thor SS Bass or maybe

the Thunder N' Lightning Bird Bass. Are

you familiar with those two at all? What

do you think of them?"

Elvis answers Bill's questions in full detail, helping Bill begin to learn what Elvis wants and how he can help him get it. Next, Bill continues to keep Elvis involved in the dialogue, while directing the tactical conversation needed to build the sale with his reply here:

      Employee: *"OK cool, cool I got you. I am definitely*

                     familiar with both of those Basses. I don't

own them but I have played them both

before. Your situation is one that I can

definitely help you out with, dude, as I

also play Bass. I have some follow up

questions though. What bass sound are

you looking for the tracks to have? Also,

are you a teenager? Younger than that?

Adult? You don't sound like a kid, but I

just want to make sure first."

In his reply on the previous page, Bill subtly moves into step three of the upselling formula (create assurance) when Bill makes the comment, "Your situation is one that I can definitely help you with, dude, as I also play Bass." Immediately afterwards, he continues the dialogue while directing the tactical conversation, as there is still more specific information that Bill needs to build a sale. Knowing this, Bill skillfully asks Elvis, "What bass sound are you looking for the tracks to have? Also, are you a teenager? Younger than that? Adult? You don't sound like a kid, but I just want to make sure first." Elvis then replies, answering Bill's questions with:

Customer: *"OK Awesome. Yeah man. I'm in college.*

20 years old. The Bass sound I'm looking

for is similar to that old Motown sound."

The reply from Elvis telling Bill that he is in college, 20 years old that he is looking for that old Motown sound gives Bill all the information he needs to direct the conversation towards a sale. Bill continues the dialogue and tactical conversation with this reply:

> Employee: *"OK that's cool. Perfect. Here are my*
>
> *thoughts and advice on everything that*
>
> *you just mentioned based on my skills and*
>
> *experience..."*

With Bill's reply above, he subtly utilizes step three (create assurance) again when he tells Elvis "based on my skills and experience" then Bill transitions into step four (describe) when he begins to talk to Elvis about the Terrible Thor Bass and the Thunder N Lightning Bird when he continues the dialogue below:

> Employee: *"... The Ivan Terrible Thor SS Bass is an*
>
> *alright Bass, especially at a price of*
>
> *$175.95; however, this Bass is kind of*
>
> *small as it is meant more for a younger*
>
> *musician. I think if you were to purchase*
>
> *this Bass the compact size would make it*
>
> *more difficult for you to play being that it*
>
> *will probably be uncomfortable. I've tried*
>
> *playing one before myself, and while it is*

a good beginner Bass for a younger musician, the size limits its capabilities; for example, it is harder to play slap on it given the compact size and location of the pickups on the body. As far as the Thunder N' Lightning Bird Bass. This Bass rocks! I absolutely love it. It is comfortable, looks cool, and sounds good. The reason that I do not own it is because it produces a very specific tone that I don't really need. Also, while the description of the instrument states that it is made of a maple neck. If you look at picture three on the website, you will notice that the maple neck is stained so it closely matches the color of the rosewood fingerboard. While this looks great in appearance, given your situation of trying to learn songs quickly, I think that this Bass will take you longer to become comfortable and adjusted to

> *fretting the notes as accurately and*
>
> *quickly as possible based on the design of*
>
> *the neck. Also, this Bass is not really*
>
> *known for that old Motown sound that*
>
> *you are going for..."*

Bill has described (step 4) in very specific detail his thoughts on why he would not recommend these instruments to Elvis based on what is he trying to accomplish. This is where the strategy of storytelling that we talked about in chapter two helps, because Bill is basically telling a true story about his experiences with these instruments. In his reply above, Bill continues to direct the tactical conversation using storytelling combined with step four (describe) and introducing lesson four (you need to learn how to present the sale to customer) from chapter one- how to be great at sales. Bill continues the dialogue below, still utilizing the strategies of step four (describe) and lesson four (how to present the sale...). Bill continues with his suggestion of the Standard Precise Bass, which we read about here:

> *Employee:*   *"...With all of that being said, I would like*
>
>   *to suggest and ask you to take a look at*
>
>   *the Bass called the Standard Precise. This*
>
>   *was the Bass that was used on the old*
>
>   *Motown tunes and it will give you the*
>
>   *sound that you're looking for..."*

When Bill states, "This was the Bass that was used on the old Motown tunes and it will give you the sound that you're looking for." he is transitioning from step four (describe) into step five (awake desire). This also builds on Bill's knowledge of lessons two, three, and four from how to be great at sales. By learning what Elvis wanted (lesson two), followed by the effective questions that he asked and tactical conversation, which are helping prepare the sale (lesson three), now Bill is transitioning to lesson four (how to present the sale to the customer). Bill continues the sales dialogue with the following:

Employee: *"...Now I know that you're seeing that the*

cost is $624.99, which may seem out of

your budget, but this will actually work to

your advantage- here is how; right now

the cost of the Thunder N Lightning Bird is

$349.99 and when you add tax you were

probably planning on spending close to

$400 even with the free shipping. I can

save you over $300 in your pocket today

if you wanted to take advantage of this

opportunity. Right now, we are offering a

limited time special finance offer on the

Standard Precise Bass where if you

purchase this Bass in any one of the five

color options then you can pay off the

Bass within 36 months including 0%

interest..."

When Bill mentions the cost of the Standard Precise Bass, he immediately follows with, "this will actually work to your advantage." Next, he describes the benefits of what Elvis almost spent ($400), then he mentions the benefit of free shipping, followed by, "I can save you over $300 in your pocket today if you wanted to take advantage of this opportunity." With this line, Bill is continuing with step five (awake desire). Then Bills explains, "Right now, we are offering a limited time special finance offer on the Standard Precise Bass..." After this statement, he mentions another benefit that this deal is available in "any one of the five color options" and then he continues with step five (awake desire) when Bill says, "you can pay off the Bass within 36 months including 0% interest." Here, Bill begins describing the finance opportunity in more detail to Elvis, continuing with step five (awake desire) and seamlessly moving into step 6 (beat their test) when Bill continues with the following specific choice of words in the dialogue continued here:

> *Employee:*   *So, while the Standard Precise Bass might*
>
> *cost more at $624.99 if you decide to take*
>
> *advantage of the special finance*
>
> *promotion that we have going on right*
>
> *now you can actually get that Bass for 36*
>
> *monthly payments of only $17.36 per*
>
> *month. So, instead of spending close to*

> *$400 on the other Bass that you were*
>
> *thinking about, you could actually get the*
>
> *Standard Precise this week with our free*
>
> *expedited shipping included and it would*
>
> *only cost you $17.36 today, saving you*
>
> *over $300 which is huge because studio*
>
> *time is expensive and that $300 savings is*
>
> *more money that you could put towards*
>
> *the budget of recording the songs for your*
>
> *Mom..."*

Bill continues with utilizing step six (beat their test). Bill restates the additional benefits of free expedited shipping, the low monthly cost of only $17.36, and how this opportunity to save money can also help Elvis accomplish his goal to help him record songs for his mom as he will now have extra money in his pocket. All of this shows lesson two from how to be great at sales that Bill has found out what Elvis wants, and he is helping him find the best way that he can get it. Bill continues the sales dialogue below:

> Employee: *"...There is a catch though that I want to*
>
>   *warn you about. The special finance*
>
>   *promotion ends in two days. This*

> *opportunity is not available every day. It*
>
> *is a limited time offer..."*

Quick note. When Bill mentions "The special finance promotion ends in two days," this is another selling technique that Bill is utilizing as he is subtly but truthfully informing Elvis that there is a sense of urgency here. Bill continues with the tactical conversation:

Employee: *"... I really think this is a great deal for*

you though as you will be saving a ton of

money and this Bass will give you the

sound that you're looking for. Plus, it's

comfortable, looks beautiful and it is well

known in the industry giving it a higher

resale value if you ever decide to sell it or

trade it in in the future for different gear.

And last, dude, if you get the Bass and find

that it is really not the instrument for you,

you are able to return the Bass to us for a

refund or store credit if you want."

Bill continues the tactical conversation with a last minute explanation and reminder of all the benefits that Elvis is getting here; great deal, saving a ton of money, this Bass will give him the sound that he is looking for, the Bass is comfortable, beautiful, higher resale value, and easy return system if Elvis doesn't like the Bass. All these statements are last minute efforts to create assurance, describe, awake desire, and beat Elvis's test (steps three, four, five, and six), which are going to lead up to step seven (call to action) in just a moment when Bill says this:

> Employee: *"... It's a very simple process, but based on*
>
> *what you told me I really believe you're*
>
> *going to like this Bass and it is the right*
>
> *one for you. Would you like to purchase*
>
> *the Standard Precise Bass for only 36*
>
> *monthly payments of $17.36?"*

Here are the final steps. Bill gives one last effort to create assurance and beat any test when Bill states, "It's a very simple process, but based on what you told me I really believe you're going to like this Bass and it is the right one for you." Bill then transitions into step seven (call to action) when he asks, "Would you like to purchase the standard precise bass for only 36 monthly payments of $17,36?" After presenting the call to action, Bill is in step 8 (decision time) when he pauses the conversation to let Elvis be the next to speak:

> Customer: *"Holy smokes! Absolutely, I want that*
>
> *deal. This sounds great, man!"*

The reply from Elvis above finishes the successful upsell opportunity #1. Bill easily could have made a smaller sale when Elvis stated that he was interested in the Thunder N Lightning Bird Bass as that was a very cool instrument, but instead, Bill used his music knowledge along with his sales skills and experience to create upsell opportunity #1 to an instrument that will help Elvis better accomplish his goals. To summarize this sale, Bill effectively demonstrated all eight steps from the upselling advantage formula, combined with storytelling from chapter two, and he especially utilized all five lessons from chapter one, where we learned how to be great at sales. Finally, Bill proved to us that "The only way to earn money is by providing people with services or products which are needed and useful."[7]

After Bill completes the initial sale, he quickly jumps back to lesson three from chapter one- how to be great at sales, as Bill continues to direct a tactical conversation with Elvis, subtly bringing to conversation opportunity #2 for upselling that we read next.

Opportunity #2 for upsell– new case for the Bass

In opportunity #2 for upsell, Bill continues lesson three from how to be great at sales when he is preparing the sale through directing a tactical conversation. Bill also rewinds to step one of the upselling advantage formula (attention please) to begin upsell opportunity #2 right after Elvis purchased his new Bass. Bill continues the conversation here:

> *Employee:*   *"Yeah dude, it really is a super deal. You made the right call and really lucked out with the timing to pick up this Bass now. I just have a couple of more questions..."*

Bill begins upsell opportunity #2, heading right back to his how to be great at sales training when he continues to direct a tactical conversation (lesson three) and brings the conversation right back to step one (attention please) of the 8 step upselling advantage. Bill first reassures and compliments Elvis that he just got a great deal, made the right decision, and was lucky to call when he did, helping validate his purchase decision and making Elvis feel great and excited about the choice he just made. Immediately after these compliments, Bill then says, "I just have a couple of more questions." Here Bill grabs the attention of Elvis, so they're back to step one (attention please) when Bill says:

> Employee: "...We also have cases for the Standard
>
> Precise Bass- I wanted to mention this as
>
> you sound like a talented musician and
>
> talented musicians are usually very smart
>
> and they also are very protective of their
>
> instruments..."

After catching the attention of Elvis when Bill tells him that he has a couple of more questions, Bill jumps into step two (be interesting) of the 8 step upselling advantage when he says "...We also have cases for the Standard Precise Bass. I wanted to mention this as you sound like a talented musician and talented musicians are usually very smart and they also are very protective of their instruments..." This is important because if Bill had just asked Elvis "if he wanted to buy a case too?" then he would have presented step 1 (attention please) then gone straight to steps 7 and 8 (call to action and decision time). Bill does not do this though; instead, he moves into the correct next step of be interesting (step 2). Once onto step two, Bill then utilizes the persuasion theory of altercasting, which we talked about earlier.

Remember, "the goal of altercasting is to project an identity on your audience that is congruent with one's own goals, meaning the goal of your audience."[23] In this example, Bill subtly uses altercasting on Elvis when he makes the compliment of: "I wanted to mention this as you sound like a talented musician and talented musicians are usually very smart and they also are very protective of their instruments..." Here, just like the goal of altercasting states, Bill tells Elvis that he sounds like a talented musician. Then Bill says to Elvis that talented musicians are usually very smart and they are also very protective of their instruments..." Bill's compliment in the form of an observation projects the identity that Elvis is talented and projects that image that most other talented musicians who are smart are also very protective of their instruments. This is an image that would be congruent with the goals of Elvis, as he is going to be traveling back and forth to the studio. Bill reminds him of this in the tactical conversation next when Bill says:

> *Employee:*   *"...A case would definitely help you protect*
>
> *your Bass when you are traveling back*
>
> *and forth to the studio..."*

This statement moves Bill into step three (create assurance), then right afterwards, Bill continues the 8 step formula when he says:

> *Employee:*   *"...and if you ever decided to resell in the*
>
> *future you'll be protecting your*
>
> *investment by purchasing a case. Cases*
>
> *for the Standard Precise Bass only cost*
>
> *$99.99...and you can finance that along*

with the Bass as a package so if you added

on the case, instead of $17.36, the new

monthly payment would only be $20.14

for 36 months. It is only an extra $2.78 a

month."

Bills continues to create assurance (step three) when he says, "and if you ever decide to resell in the future you'll be protecting your investment by purchasing a case." After this statement, it is time for Bill to move into step 4 (describe) when he says, "Cases for the Standard Precise Bass only cost $99.99..." Next, in the same sentence, Bill moves into step five (awake desire) when he tells Elvis, "and you can finance that along with   the Bass as a package." Again, in the same sentence, Bill tactically directs the conversation into step six (beat their test) to remove any skepticism or concern that Elvis might have when Bill says, "so if you added on the case, instead of $17.36, the new monthly payment would only be $20.14 for 36 months. It is only an extra $2.78 a month." Having the math already figured out for Elvis helps him make an easier decision, thinking, "It is only an extra $2.78 a month. I spend more than that on coffee (or something similar)," hoping this thought justifies purchasing the case right now, as it is a great deal and Elvis should go for it. Bill then moves into steps 7 and 8 (call to action and decision time) when Bills says:

Employee: "...To me, this is a no brainer to help

protect your investment and another

excellent deal for you. Do you want to

purchase the case also?

(Pause. Bill lets the customer be the next to speak).

Here are the final steps. Bill gives one last effort to create assurance and beat any test when Bill states, "To me, this is a no brainer to help protect your investment and another excellent deal for you." Bill then transitions into step seven (call to action) when he asks, "Do you want to purchase the case also?" After presenting the call to action, Bill is in step 8 (decision time) when he pauses the conversation to let Elvis be the next to speak.

Customer: *"Good thinking. Yes, I'll add on the case*

also."

The reply from Elvis above finishes the successful upsell opportunity #2. Here, Bill easily could have just ended the call after the sale of the Standard Precise Bass, but instead, he had a script thought out ahead of time of contingency plans that consisted of other music gear he might be able to sell along with the Bass. The contingency plans and sales script were all based on his music knowledge, combined with his sales skills and experience, to create the chance to sell Elvis a new case also. Once again, Bill proved to us that "The only way to earn money is by providing people with services or products which are needed and useful." [7]

After Bill completes the upsell opportunity #2 sale, he quickly jumps back to lesson three from chapter one- how to be great at sales, as Bill continues to direct a tactical conversation with Elvis subtly bringing to conversation opportunity #3 for upselling that we read next.

Opportunity #3 for upsell– Flatwound Strings for the Bass

Following a similar technique that he used in opportunity #2, in opportunity #3 for upsell, Bill continues lesson three from how to be great at sales when he is preparing the sale through directing a tactical conversation. Bill also rewinds to step one of the upselling advantage formula (attention please) to begin upsell opportunity #3 right after Elvis has purchased the new case. Bill continues the conversation here:

> Employee: *"Smart move, dude. I would've done the*
>
> *same thing if I were in your shoes. OK so*
>
> *that was question one; the second*
>
> *question that I wanted to ask you was..."*

Bill begins upsell opportunity #3, heading right back to his how to be great at sales training when he continues to direct a tactical conversation (lesson three) and brings the conversation right back to step one (attention please) of the 8 step upselling advantage. Bill first reassures and compliments Elvis that he just got a great deal, made the right decision, and that Bill also would had made the same decision if he were in his shoes, making Elvis feel great and excited about the choice he just made. Immediately after these compliments, Bill then says, "OK so that was question one; the second question that I wanted to ask you was..." Here, Bill grabs the attention of Elvis, so they're back to step one (attention please). Then Bill transitions into step two (be interesting) when he says:

> Employee: *"...you said that you were going for the old*
>
> *Motown sound. The Standard Precise*

> *Bass comes stock with roundwound*
>
> *strings; however, I'm not sure how much*
>
> *you've read about on the classic Motown*
>
> *sound but the Bass players on those*
>
> *records all used flatwound strings on their*
>
> *Standard Precise Basses. I highly*
>
> *recommend that you add flatwounds to*
>
> *your new Bass..."*

Bill talks to Elvis about how the Bass players used flatwound strings in step two (be interesting), and then he recommends to Elvis that he adds flatwounds to his new Bass. Immediately after this recommendation, Bill moves on to step three (create assurance) when Bill says, "They are more comfortable to play." Bill then moves onto step four(describe) when he tells Elvis "and give you that true sound that you're looking for, so the songs will sound their absolute best for your mom." Bill then moves onto step five (awake desire) when he says:

> Employee: *"...If you wanted to add a set they are only*
>
> *$34.99 for a 4 string set but again if you*
>
> *purchase these today we can add them in*
>
> *on the finance package..."*

Bill then quickly moves into step six (beat their test) when he attempts to remove any concern about the price increase by stating:

> *Employee:* "...so if you picked up the flatwound set also your cost would only increase by 97 cents a month to just $21.11..."

Next, Bill continues on explaining step six (beat their test) by restating all the benefits of the sale, directing the tactical conversation and preparing the sale to move into steps 7 and 8 (call to action and decision time).

> *Employee:* "...That includes everything, dude, the Standard Precise Bass, the new case, and the new set of flatwound strings. I can have all 3 of these items out to you and on your doorstep in 2-3 days if you want to go for the deal now..."

While Bill is doing all of this, he again references chapter two and utilizes the power of storytelling in his scales script. Bill begins his storytelling when he mentions the following:

> *Employee:* "...Plus, most importantly, dude, it's for your Mom, not only will she think you sound great on the record but you'll also have personal satisfaction of success knowing you recorded the best sound possible with this gear. That feeling is

> *totally worth it especially when you look*
>
> *back and it only cost you an extra 97 cents*
>
> *a month..."*

After the storytelling, restating the benefits, and preparing the sale, Bill is now ready to present the sale and move into steps 7 and 8 (call to action and decision time) when he says:

Employee"   *"...Do you want to add the flatwound*

strings also to your order?"

(Pause. Bill lets the customer be the next to speak).

Customer: *"Oh my goodness, you're exactly right. I*

almost forgot about the flatwound strings

on the Motown Bass sound. Thanks for

reminding me. Yes, absolutely I want

them. Heavy gauge please."

The reply from Elvis above finishes successful upsell opportunity #3. Again, Bill easily could have just ended the call after the sale of the Standard Precise Bass and the new case, but instead, he had a script thought out ahead of time of contingency plans that consisted of other music gear he might be able to sell. The contingency plans and sales script were based on his music knowledge, combined with his sales skills and experience when he learned what Bill was looking for and how he could help him get it. In this instance, meaning the old Motown sound, Bill utilized lesson two from chapter one in how to be great at sales when Bill remembered, "The most important secret of salesmanship is to find out what the other fellow wants, then help him find the best way to get it." [8] When Bill was able to accomplish this, he was also able to prove to us once again that "The only way to earn money is by providing people with services or products which are needed and useful." [7]

Next, once again, right after Bill completes the upsell opportunity #3, he quickly jumps back to lesson three from chapter one- how to be great at sales, as Bill continues to direct a tactical conversation with Elvis subtly bringing to conversation opportunity #4 for upselling that we read next.

Opportunity #4 for upsell– A Bass Amp for Elvis

> Employee: *"Cool, Cool. Sounds good, Elvis. I actually*
>
> *just have one more question that I just*
>
> *thought of... Jamerson used to play with a*
>
> *classic B-15 amp to get that old Motown*
>
> *sound..."* [37]

Here, Bill right away heads back to step one (attention please) when he says, "I actually just have one more question that I just thought of..." Then in the middle of the sentence, Bill immediately moves onto step two (be interesting) as he begins to say, "Jamerson used to play with a classic B-15 amp to get that old Motown sound..." Unfortunately, this would be as far Bill would get in upsell opportunity #4. Sometimes, there are unknown variables beyond our control, like we talked about in chapter five in the troubleshooting guide and also saw earlier during the Devil Daves Bloody Mary Script Analysis, when the customer simply declined because he didn't like tomato juice. A similar incident happens to Bill here in upsell opportunity #4 when Bill learns that Elvis doesn't need a Bass amp, because he already has a keyboard amp to practice with, and the studio has one on site for him when it is time to record. Bill handles the rejection professionally and simply says:

> Employee: *"Haha. Awesome, man. OK cool, you've*
>
> *already thought of that then. Good glad to*
>
> *hear that that plan is going to work out*
>
> *for you..."*

At this point, Bill is satisfied with the results of his upselling attempts, and he decides to move the sale to the final purchases stages. Bill has completed the tactical conversation and directed the sale wonderfully.

     The end of the conversation occurs with Bill telling Elvis, "...Thanks for calling us. I'm going to email you a copy of the receipt. If there's anything else I can help you with don't hesitate to call me back..." This leaves Elvis thinking that he was in control of the experience and the phone call is finished. Bill however knows that, in a few months, he will follow up with Elvis to see how the recording went and how that Bass worked for him, and maybe even let him know about an upcoming sale, because when Elvis first called Bill today, Bill had a very specific greeting:

> Employee: *"Good afternoon! This is your sales*
>
> *engineer Bill speaking. How can I help*
>
> *you?"*

When Bill uses the title sales engineer, this helps establish authority. He is showing that he knows what he is talking about. Bill has already established that this is going to be a long-term relationship, and he has set himself a contingency plan here for future sales. This is possible because Bill has learned how to prepare the sale to the customer, and Bill knew from reading <u>The 8 Step Upselling Advantage</u> when to utilize the strategies of storytelling, altercasting, and the value of using a script. Last, Bill also knew from reading <u>The 8 Step Upselling Advantage</u> that "The only way to earn money is by providing people with services or products which are needed and useful."[7]

In chapter one, we learned from Rick Noel that "A typical path to purchase, whether Business to Business (B2B) or Business to Consumer (B2C), typically includes the following four stages: Awareness > Consideration >> Intent >>> Decision." [11]

Bill's sale to Elvis showed these four stages exactly as Rick described they would happen. Bill not only was successful in making the sale, but the next time Elvis needs music gear, he will think to call or e-mail Bill first based on his experience today.

Chapter 7

More Tips to Help You Learn The 8 Step Upselling Advantage

In the beginning of this book, you were greeted with the opportunity to read two introduction letters. The first letter was addressed to Restaurant Owners and Managers, and the second letter was addressed to Bartenders, Servers, and Staff. Inside the letter to bartenders, servers, and staff, you probably recall a section telling you about the "worst jobs in America" article and how over 20% of that list were jobs in the restaurant and food industry. For a majority of this book, the strategies and techniques have been presented to you under the assumption that you're a bartender, waiter, or waitress. For this chapter, though, I am going to change direction and talk under the assumption that you're a delivery driver. Remember from the list of "Worst jobs in America" that Driver/Sales workers was #22 on the list, so I would like to include part of this book where they get a chance to be the main character also. Please note that the tips that will be presented in the beginning of this chapter could also possibly work very well for servers and bartenders as well. Last, in the second half of this chapter are going to be more tips addressed to servers; however, these tips could work well for delivery drivers also.

In this chapter, I am going to present the opportunity that delivery drivers have to upsell and how delivery drivers can use it to learn the eight step upselling advantage formula. Additionally, through these examples, I hope you discover a customized method while reading the chapter that will encourage and excite you, in turn benefiting you in additional ways besides the ideas mentioned here.

The first thing I would like to recommend is that delivery drivers help answer the phone to take orders and learn how to upsell with the eight step upselling advantage formula. The reason I say this is because delivery drivers especially have potential to become very good at this skill. Also, if you recognize the opportunity that you have in front of you, you could immediately benefit financially from learning the eight step upselling advantage, along with these extra tips and techniques.

When delivery drivers are answering the phones, not only do they have the benefit of using the eight step upselling advantage formula, but sometimes, they also have the opportunity to increase their own tips for the night, simply from answering the phone. One example describing this method that occurs often is when you're dealing with a regular customer that routinely orders the same exact item every time, and the employee (driver) is using a POS system to take the order. When the delivery driver answers the phone and they know that the customer gets the same sandwich each time they order, instead of having the customer repeat the order, tell the customer exactly what they are getting, but do this by asking them a question. You're not going to just say, "I think you're going to have a Roast Beef sandwich." Instead, use the opportunity to present a question in the style of "Would you like a Roast Beef sandwich, cold, with light lettuce, tomato, onions, and extra mayo today?" Now you know that you're just guessing that the customer is going to be getting the same item as last time. But, when you do this, there are two possible answers that occur frequently when a customer is asked this question: 1) The customer is going to give you one of two possible replies as an answer. First, regardless of their decision, they usually laugh because they think that, because they order so much, the restaurant has their favorite item memorized. Then they are either going to say, "Nope. I'm going to switch it up today and have something else instead." Or 2) They are going to say, "Yup. That is exactly what I want." Sometimes, when the customer is amazed, they'll ask, "How did you know?" or they'll say something along the lines of "Wow that's exactly what I had last time! I can't believe you remembered that!"

This benefits your restaurant by giving the impression that you take extra care in making sure the customer's food is exactly the way they want it. This immediately is satisfying to the customer, because they're already getting the feeling that their food is going to be perfect and made exactly how they like it. The customer that recognizes this detail will remember to call your establishment in the future, as they know what to expect and appreciate your attention to detail. Now how do you get your driver to see that this opportunity can be used greatly to their advantage?

When the customer laughs after recognizing the attention to detail and being amazed at the exactness of every little detail that your establishment puts into preparing the customer's food, naturally given your employee's excellent customer service skills, they will laugh along with the employee. As I said earlier in chapter 4, the combination of smiling and enjoying what should have been a simple generic phone call has the customer associating your restaurant with appreciation and remembering how personable the staff is. Not only will they think of you next time they are hungry, but we are also helping to develop the employee's customer service skills, and hopefully, the customers will suggest their friends eat at your restaurant also. This is important in many ways in terms of customer satisfaction and exceptional customer service skills, and the most creative and the most intelligent employees will take this opportunity a step further. This opportunity is where delivery drivers can really benefit financially if you recognize the chance to seize the opportunity that you have in front of you.

After the driver guesses what the customer wants and if they get a reply that is similar to "How did you know?" the driver then has two options. They can reply with a standard, "We have a POS system that states order history when we punch in your phone number." Or, the driver can be creative with their reply by saying something along the lines of: "It was a lucky guess" or "Actually I took your order last time and remembered what you ordered." Either one of these replies will get a welcomed and amazed response. After this conversation occurs, the employee can begin to utilize the eight step upselling advantage formula to try to get the customer to add a soda or another product to their order.

Now using the same example, if the Roast Beef sandwich ordered previously was exactly what the customer wanted this time, and he or she also wanted the sandwich delivered, the delivery driver who answered the phone and recognized the opportunity presented would be smart to reply something along the lines of, "Actually, it was a psychic intuition. That's why the Boss pays me the big bucks." Then carry on the conversation as if it was a normal order.

Later, when the delivery driver delivers the sandwich to the customer after giving the customer their order, having the customer pay for it, and hopefully give a tip, before the delivery driver leaves the house, tell the delivery drivers to refer back to their original conversation on the phone with the customer. Here's how to do this. Right before the customer thinks you are leaving, simply say to the customer something along the lines of: "Oh yeah, in case you were wondering, I'm the one who answered the phone, my name is _____, nice to meet you." The driver can then tell them how they knew of the customer's order, or if the customer does not ask, the driver does not have to mention it. The reason you're having the driver do all of this is because it brings the customer back to the original phone call when they placed the order and how much they enjoyed the experience. Sometimes, the customer will have enjoyed it so much and appreciate the thoughtfulness that the customer will give the driver a second tip in addition to the one they just gave them literally two minutes prior. Now sometimes, this method works, and sometimes, it doesn't in terms of the delivery driver getting an additional tip, but with a little effort and practice, delivery drivers really do have the potential to make extra money if they become very good at this skill.

The main objective of this exercise is to get the employee comfortable and developing their own style when upselling. Again, once the employee gets comfortable taking orders on the phone and learns how much "fun" it is to answer the phone, they'll soon begin to think of other ways on their own to increase sales.

This strategy is also especially beneficial to delivery drivers around holiday times. For example, if it is Halloween and the driver is delivering to a party, it is not uncommon for the delivery driver to end up with a tip that consists of money, donuts, apple cider, and candy all from the same house. Also, if it is Christmas and people are feeling extra generous, delivery drivers can use this to their advantage, combined with the information that we have discussed so far in this chapter, and see that their tips are larger just because of the time of year and with people being in a giving spirit. However, these opportunities are only possible if the drivers recognize the opportunity in front of them and how they can benefit financially from learning the eight step upselling advantage formula and answering the phone.

I highly encourage your delivery drivers to help answer the phone to take orders and learn how to upsell, especially using the eight step upselling advantage formula. In addition, I hope the examples I just described above also will help encourage delivery drivers to take full advantage of the opportunity they have in front of them.

Now for the rest of the staff, here are some separate methods to get everyone involved and interested in learning the eight step upselling advantage formula that are going to benefit them as well. Your delivery drivers can participate in these methods as well, considering they will be open to the entire staff.

The second half of this chapter is going to present more tips and strategies that are specifically for all current restaurant owners, managers, and shift supervisors, or for anyone who hopes to advance to one of these roles in the future.

To help increase staff participation in utilizing, practicing, and honing their newly learned skill of the eight step upselling advantage, every month have an "upsell item of the month contest" open to the entire staff. Pick one item from your menu, and for that month, whoever sells the most of that item wins a prize or cash bonus to give them an incentive. You can have the item be something that is relatively new to your menu, or they can be common items that sell every day, something specific like 2-liter bottles of soda. This contest can be entirely optional to participate, but to encourage your employees to participate, make a big chart that has every employee's name on it and have an end of the week tally, so the staff can see how they are doing, who is winning, and what place they are in. In addition to the cash bonus or prize that everyone would be interested in wanting to win, this will encourage your staff to participate and try harder to be the winner. There are variations to this type of contest, but the one above is my personal favorite and the one that I think is the easiest to organize and keep track of. The other exciting thing about this contest is that the manager or owner of the store can see exactly what employees might need more encouragement or coaching on upselling. In addition, they will be able to see which employees are the most enthusiastic and creative.

For example, it is the last week of the monthly contest, and Ozzie sees that he is in second place, having sold 41 orders of garlic knots this month. Ozzie is right behind Will, who has sold 50 orders, with the closest employee next to them in third place being Izzie (pronounced "Is He"), who has only sold 17. Ozzie only needs nine more orders of garlic knots to catch Will. Ozzie also knows that Will is going on vacation on Wednesday, which gives him Thursday, Friday, and Saturday in his favor to try to pass Will to win the $100 cash bonus for the month. The interesting part in this scenario for you, as the manager or owner, will be to see what Ozzie does in this situation. Will he offer to work extra hours in an effort to beat Will? Will Ozzie not offer to pick up the extra hours and just rely on his normal hours to try to beat Will? Or will he take full advantage of the situation by: 1) Offering to work extra hours, or 2) Recognizing the $100 cash bonus, will Ozzie decide to order ten orders of garlic knots for himself to boost his own sales on top of those nights' sales? In essence, with option 2, he has guaranteed himself to be the winner. Even though he spent $40 on ten orders of garlic knots, with there being a $100 cash bonus, Ozzie is still making an extra $60 for that month. Plus, the best part about it is that Ozzie gets to eat 120 garlic knots for dinner on Friday and Saturday.

Last, regardless of who wins the monthly contests or which delivery driver makes the most money, participating staff can benefit from using the methods above to teach and encourage your employees about the value in learning and mastering the skill of the eight step upselling advantage formula.

As a result of the hard work and dedication from your employees, and through proper coaching and encouragement from your management team, your restaurant, its sales, and your staff will all benefit from full employee and staff participation.

Through practicing the suggestions mentioned so far in this book, working on your skills by doing something as simple as studying the menu so you are more comfortable with it, listening to "The Strangest Secret" by Earl Nightingale, or challenging yourself to master the eight step upselling advantage, you will ultimately accomplish the feat of having mastered the skill of learning the eight step upselling advantage formula and how to upsell.

The next chapter talks about my favorite tip and strategy that I'm going to teach you. Chapter 8 is going to teach you The Best Place to Learn The 8 Step Upselling Advantage. Now, let's learn more about where the best place to learn the 8 step upselling advantage actually is.

Chapter 8
The Best Place to Learn
The 8 Step Upselling Advantage

In 1825, a man named Elisha Judson left his home in the settlement of Kingsboro, New York, and with a cartload full of leather gloves and mittens, he headed for Boston, Massachusetts.[38]

For well over 20 years prior, in post American Revolutionary War times, the upstate New York settlements of Kingsboro, McNab Mills, and Throopville began manufacturing their own leather apparel as a necessity of life. They were able to accomplish this thanks to the availability of deerskins, the purity and abundance of water, and hemlock bark for the tanning process. [38] The tanning process prevents the rotting of animal skins when they are wet, making the skins strong, pliable, and waterproof. Hemlock bark was used because it contained more tannin than the other northern trees in the Adirondack Mountains.[39] The geological advantages of deerskins, water, and hemlock bark prompted some to specialize in the tanning and dressing of leather, and as a result of these efforts, they created deerskin apparel, including mittens and gloves. [38] These leather products would prove to be valuable in trade with other communities. Six weeks later, Elisha Judson returned from his trip. Mr. Judson sold all the mittens and gloves while he was in Boston and returned home to Kingsboro with an empty cart and $600 in silver, the equivalent of about one year's wages. [38]

To the communities of Kingsboro, Throopville, and McNab Mills, it was evident that glove making could be a source of greater wealth in a wider market in places such as Boston and New York City. Shortly afterwards, when the first post office was established, McNab Mills was officially renamed Gloversville.[38]

Young Gloversville grew and eventually expanded to include the neighboring settlements of Kingsboro and Throopville. By 1853, when Gloversville received its first charter as a village, the population was 1,318 people.

According to the 1860 census, that was the year when the profitability in glove making was at its peak for the area. "The smallest shops, those producing under $5,000 a year, reported an average profit of 44% above the cost of raw materials and wages. The slightly larger shops, producing between $5,000 and $10,000 annually, were the least profitable, but still reported almost 41%."

"As production grew, profits soared, reaching an average of 81% for shops producing over $30,000 worth of gloves. These profits are so grand that in many instances one year's profit exceeded the total capital investment." [40]

To put that into perspective in terms of operational accomplishments, "Alanson Judson, who emerged in 1860 with the largest glove-making operation in Gloversville, converted 22,000 deerskins into 4,200 dozen gloves with the help of 11 male employees and 50 women. The largest in Johnstown, Russell & Gilbert, employed 58 women and 12 men to produce 4,500 dozen gloves from 18,500 deerskins. Of the 69 firms in the (1860) census, 24 produced over 1,000 dozen gloves annually, 28 employed more than 10 females." [40]

Meanwhile, as the world was heading towards the end of the 19th century and as the communities in Gloversville and Johnstown were making gloves in upstate NY, around that same time there was a reunion of the soldiers happening in the state of Massachusetts. Attending this reunion were soldiers who were part of the Forty-sixth Massachusetts Regiment. They all had served together in the American Civil War. At the reunion, a Captain, named Russell Conwell, gave a speech to his fellow soldiers. It was a mere accidental address, and afterwards, Conwell had no intentions to give it again. However, word spread, and the lecture committees soon began calling, leading

Russell Conwell out on the road where he would eventually deliver that original address over 6,152 times. Conwell called his speech "Acres of Diamonds." [41, 42]

"Acres of Diamonds" is full of inspiration, suggestions, and aid. However, Conwell would alter it prior to every speech to meet the local circumstances for the thousands of different places where he delivered it. He would accomplish this by arriving to the towns early, and prior to giving his lecture, he would talk with the locals about their individual communities, the opportunities their towns presented, as well as its accomplishments and failures. Then he would customize his speech to include the local circumstances. However, the base of the speech would remain the same, as it was designed to help "every person, of either sex, who cherishes the high resolve of sustaining a career of usefulness and honor." [41]

According to Conwell, "Where you are is who you are…The time never came in the history of the world when you could get rich so quickly manufacturing without capital as you can now…'Acres of Diamonds' -the idea- has continuously been precisely the same. The idea is that in this country of ours every man has the opportunity to make more of himself than he does in his own environment, with his own skill, with his own energy, and with his own friends." [41]

This attitude and the lessons that "Acres of Diamonds" taught are precisely what was happening in Gloversville and Johnstown, NY at the same time beginning in the late 18th century. The communities in those early settlements realized, just as Conwell said, "…man has the opportunity to make more of himself than he does in his own environment, with his own skill, with his own energy, and with his own friends." [41]

The communities of Gloversville and Johnstown utilized their own environment's abundance of water, deerskins, and hemlock bark, when combined with their own skills and energies, and they were able to create leather apparel, specifically gloves and mittens, which were valued and desired in the rest of the country.

Remember the area wasn't exactly popular or booming when they first began. Elisha Judson first went to Boston in 1825, and it wasn't until 1852 that the village of Gloversville was first established when the population soared to 1,318 people. Rev. Homer N. Dunning gives us a closer look describing the village of Gloversville at the time. Rev. Dunning spoke of his first experiences in Gloversville during a speech he gave in 1892 when he addressed his audience and said:

> *"In 1852 when I first came here, the population was, by the enumeration taken on September 27 of that year, 1,318. The number of houses was 250. It was incorporated on the fourteenth of January 1853... It was a community of families, mostly living each in its own house, in unusual comfort and even luxury; the people manufacturing their own goods in their own houses or on their own premises... There were almost no really poor people in the place; perhaps one reason was that there were no liquor saloons tolerated. The fact that all were engaged in the same business, while it provoked some jealousies and rivalries, nevertheless created a kinship and community of feeling; and the isolation of the place developed a strong feeling of local pride and public spirit. The travel abroad in the sale of goods also sharpened up the wits of its businessmen and brought back new ideas and stimulus to enterprise and improvement. The community, though small, was full of vitality and vigor and of ambition and faith in the future growth and development of the place. Almost everybody attended church regularly, twice or even three times a day; the prayer meetings were well attended; there was little open immorality or vice..."* [38]

Gloversville's own "Acres of Diamonds" continued to grow, and between 1890 and 1950, the city supplied nearly 90 percent of all gloves sold in the United States. [43]

The communities of Gloversville and Johnstown, NY proved Russell Conwell's theory and advice correct when he lectured across the nation, teaching his audiences, "...Where you are, is who you are...The time never came in the history of the world when you could get rich so quickly manufacturing without capital as you can now. ... Every man has the opportunity to make more of himself than he does in his own environment, with his own skill, with his own energy, and with his own friends." [41]

Now I know that 1825 was a long time ago, and there is probably a good chance that today more than 1,318 people are living in the same town or city where you live. Russell Conwell's speech is well over 100 years old, so what exactly can you manufacture without capital for yourself today?

The answer to this question is simply this. Right now, you have the skills and the opportunity to manufacture your own 8 Step Upselling Advantage script, without capital, in your own environment, and with your own energies, just like Conwell said, but where is the best place to learn the 8 Step Upselling Advantage? Where should you write your own script for yourself?

The best place to learn the 8 Step Upselling Advantage is in your own backyard and community, wherever you are now. Find a job in a restaurant, pizzeria, a Chinese food place, or at a fast food place, whatever type of food establishment that exists where you could get hired as a cashier, waiter, waitress, bartender, delivery driver, or even a supervisor, simply wherever you could see yourself enjoying the work and people. Right there is where you will have your very own best place to learn the 8 Step Upselling Advantage, and right there is where you will have the chance to practice composing your own 8 Step Upselling Advantage script and honing your skills and talents in live sales situations.

This is your opportunity to make more of yourself in your own environment, with your own skills and energies, and possibly even with your own friends.

Throughout this book, I have attempted to provide you with resources to give you as many tools as possible to help you learn the 8 Step Upselling Advantage. From learning how to be great at sales, where you read advice from Earl Nightingale, Frank Bettger, Clayton Hunsicker, Howard Litwak, and Rick Noel to learning about even more strategies, such as the value and effectiveness in storytelling from Bob Fuhr and Gerry Spence, the usefulness of altercasting, and the benefits of using a script. This all led to teaching you the actual 8 Step Upselling Advantage. That chapter and lesson was then followed with script examples, a troubleshooting guide, and how to utilize these skills in a new job or career when you feel the time is right for you, as well as additional tips to help you learn the 8 Step Upselling Advantage.

The resources and tools presented in this book were all illustrated to help guide you to the realization that, with some dedication, commitment, skill and energy, The 8 Step Upselling Advantage can also help "every person, of either sex, who cherishes the high resolve of sustaining a career of usefulness and honor."[41]

I think the best way to summarize The 8 Step Upselling Advantage is through a quote from the late Zig Ziglar. Mr. Ziglar once wrote, "The two of us (you and I) must continue on our pilgrimage by *learning, living, and looking*; learning from the past without living there; living in the present by seizing each vital moment of every single day; and looking to the future with hope, optimism, *and* education." [44]

In closing, I hope you enjoyed reading The 8 Step Upselling Advantage, and through the history lessons that I have included, I hope they helped you learn from the past without living there. I also hope this book has inspired you to want to seize each vital moment of the present, to notice opportunities available, such as learning the 8 Step Upselling Advantage, so you're able to develop and hone your own sales strategies and communication talents.

Last, I hope this book helps you recognize your own skills and that it has encouraged you to utilize your energies effectively. Through the combination of these efforts and dedication, I truly believe you can now look to the future with hope and optimism, so that you also will soon be able to recognize the Acres of Diamonds that exist nearby for you.

NFL Hall of Famer Deacon Jones once said, "It took me a long time to figure out that real big-time success comes from taking lots of small, ordinary steps in the right direction. And you can't ever take the next step until you take the first." [45, 46]

Right now, you might consider your talent and skills to be the size of small seeds; however, with perseverance and determination, you can nurture and grow your sales skills and talents when you follow the advice taught in this book. Through these lessons and your courageousness to start by taking the first step, I hope you discover that your small seeds today eventually grow up to become Acres of Money Trees.

Epilogue

A Free Gift for You...

Thank you for reading this book. I hope you found it to be interesting, and enjoyable. In closing, I have a free gift for you.

I'd like to direct you to the Great Point Publishing Silver Treasure Hunter Program. When you sign up (it's free!), you will enjoy the following benefits: Exclusive access to the Great Point Publishing Free Library. These are books published by Great Point Publishing that are available for you to download; no charge. You also get to enjoy "Free Gift" emails from Great Point Publishing. Sometimes authors utilize "free book" promotional days when they publish with Great Point Publishing and make their books available for download on amazon.com. This means their books are available at no cost to whoever wants to download them. You now also can enjoy this benefit in the future, when authors choose to utilize the free book promotional days, and their books are eligible on amazon.com. Recently hundreds of people downloaded Devil Dave's Bloody Mary Recipe Book by Ryan Pakenas when they received an email saying that Mr. Pakenas' book was available free for a limited time. You can sign up to become a Silver Treasure Hunter today on our website - www.greatpointpublishing.com. In closing, thanks again for reading and best of luck to you in your future endeavors!

Sincerely,

Christopher Hallenbeck
Great Point Publishing LLC
Gloversville, NY

More Help for Restaurant Owners & Restaurant Managers...

Some additional strategies and techniques for you

Dear Owners and Managers,

I just want to quickly share some last-minute information for you before we end this initial stage of our journey together.

During the first introduction letter, "Dear Restaurant Owners and Managers...How this book can help you increase sales..." you learned that The 8 Step Upselling Advantage is the first book in a series developed for the restaurant industry to help restaurant owners, managers, and employees increase sales, and also improve service.

At the end of the first introduction letter, you also were invited to check out increaserestaurantsales.com and sign up for our free email newsletter so you can continue to learn the latest strategies and techniques developed to help you and your shop.

I would like to encourage you to sign up for the newsletter so we can continue to help you and your staff keep your customers happy, share success stories and strategies that aim to create a public awareness of your restaurant in each of your own individual communities, and also let you know when future books in this series are released.

Thanks again for reading, I wish you the best of luck! I look forward to continuing on with the next stage of our journey together. See you on increaserestaurantsales.com!

Sincerely,

Christopher Hallenbeck
Owner
increaserestaurantsales.com

About Everett "Cubby" Faville

Everett "Cubby" Faville

"An Ode to Cubby"
By: Christopher Hallenbeck

On September 11, 2011, I was on my way to Altamont, NY with Michael Iorio and Loren Iorio to see Chuck Ragan, Street Dogs, Stiff Little Fingers, and Dropkick Murphys at The ShamRock and Roll Festival at the Altamont Fairgrounds. So, as we're heading to the show, Mike says to me:

> *"Chrit, have you ever listened to the Street Dogs?"*

> *"Nope, I missed their opening act on Thursday (9/8/2011) when I was at Fenway Park for the Street Dogs, Mighty Mighty Bosstones, and Dropkick Murphys show. I got there late right when Bosstones were going on."*

> *"O man, they're really, really good! You're going to like them a lot!"*

For the rest of the trip, Mike then proceeded to introduce me to songs by Street Dogs, and I was instantly hooked. The reason that I bring this up now is because I'm still kind of shocked at the passing of Everett Faville, who was better known to many by his childhood nickname of Cubby. I've been wanting to post something on here as a tribute to him; however, for the past week, I've kind of been at a loss for words. But then I remembered this story from 2011 and, in particular, a song Mike played for me as we were heading to Altamont that day. The song is titled "Fighter" by Street Dogs, and today, I find the lyrics appropriately describing the type of person and role model that Cubby was to me. I've added his name in parenthesis in the lyrics on the next page, and I hope you find the following as fitting as I do.

"...(Cub) soldiered on with hard work and full coffee cups. You inspired me with your tenacity. You worked hard at your trade, and people were impressed with the progress that you made. We will not forget the example you laid. Never quitting regardless of obstacles made. Hey (Cub) this one goes out to you. This is an ode to a man who spent his whole life in a fight. Never getting counted out at all or ducking from our sight. Our eulogy for him is clear, we know just what to say (Cubby Faville) was a Fighter right up to his passing day."[47]

Cubby was a fighter for his students as HFM BOCES. He truly loved his job, and I know his students truly loved him, both as a teacher and as a person. Earlier this week, I'd been working a lot trying to help the Faville Family as best as I can. But what most people don't know is that, on Monday, every time the phone rang, I didn't know if it was for the business or if it was a parent of one of Mr. Faville's students calling to see if the news was true. Sadly, I had to tell them it was, and on more than one occasion, mothers of these students instantly broke down and started crying. Mr. Faville meant that much to their kids, and Mr. Faville impacted the lives of his students in more ways than you and I can imagine or will ever know. Mr. Faville truly loved his job as the Foundations of Food teacher at BOCES, and he truly loved his students. He was a fighter for both right up to his passing day.

Cubby was a fighter for young athletes in our area as a coach at Gloversville Little League. A couple of years ago, Coach Faville and Coach Mike Bouchard worked every day with a group of young and special athletes. "Never quitting regardless of obstacles made" and fighting for a team they believed had the talent and, more importantly, the teamwork capabilities necessary to become a championship caliber team. Proudly, they all achieved this goal and won the championship two years in a row. However, this outcome very easily could have been different. The reason that I say this is because baseball is a team sport. You need the right coaches willing to fight for their team, and you need the right athletes willing to fight for their coaches. Coach Faville was that type of coach. Coach Faville was a fighter, and Coach Faville was a champion.

Last, Cubby was a fighter for his friends and family. The best way I can describe Cubby as a fighter for his friends and family is through a quote I recently learned from David Ivery. When Dave was younger, he was an Airman First Class in the United States Air Force, and during that experience, the Air Force taught him the following lesson:

"If one of you are in trouble, both of you are in trouble."

Today, Dave is a family man with a wife and three kids, and the lifelong lesson of "If one of you are in trouble, both of you are in trouble" has transcended the boundaries of Fraternal Brotherhood. Dave regularly applies this phrase as a teaching tool to help instill good morals and values in his kids' lives. He knows that, if they can grasp this concept, then they'll learn the importance of being there for each other and thinking of others before you think of yourself. Both are important qualities that anyone would want in a friend, and that every family member needs to understand and believe regardless of their age and the relationship. Dave's kids might not realize this yet, but through this mindset, they're building the foundation needed, so they can help make the world a better place to live.

When I think of my own friendship with Cubby, the best way I can describe it is that we both had an unspoken agreement that, if one of us was in trouble, both of us were in trouble. This was a core element of our friendship. Through this common belief that we shared in the importance of friends being there for each other and thinking of others before you think of yourself, I found a friend fourteen years ago when I first met Cubby Faville.

During this time, Cubby would become kind of like a father figure to me, and one of the many things he taught me is that, whenever there's calling hours, a viewing, or a wake for someone you know or someone's relative, you absolutely have to go. I quote this specifically from Cubby.

Cubby said,   *"That's when you find out who your true friends are. People might not remember everyone that was there, but they never forget who wasn't there."*

Three days ago, on December 26, 2013, over 900 friends and family members were lined up for almost five hours at Cubby Faville's wake. Some stood in line outside in the cold for almost an hour, maybe longer. They were all there to pay their final respects to a teacher, a coach, a friend, a family member, and a man who, through his morals and values, simply made their world a better place to live.

In closing, if you knew Cubby as a teacher, coach, friend, as family, or even if you're a stranger who simply respects the type of man that Cubby was, together through this small portrayal of Cubby's morals and values, we can all help make the world a better place to live. Thanks for reading this "Ode". Now, together let's bring truth to the saying, "In Loving Memory of Everett 'Cubby' Faville."

About The Author

Chris Hallenbeck lives in Gloversville, NY, a city located in the foothills of the Adirondack Mountains. In his spare time, Chris enjoys traveling, ice hockey, going to concerts, and spending time with family and friends.

Thanks and Acknowledgments

Thank you Mom, for everything. Thank you Mike, Kolin, Diana and Abbey. Thank you Olivia, Luciana, Connor, Jackson, and Finley- *you five are the best!* Thank you also especially to Cubby and Mary Jo Faville for your friendship and love, as well as your guidance in the pizza and restaurant industry. Thank you Charlie Van DeVoorde. Thank you Brian Brown. Thank you to Kelli, Jamie, Melissa and families. Thank you Brandon, Marc, Biggs, Toby, and Will. Thank you Frank DeMaio and Dr. Lana Mowdy for your help proofreading and editing this book- (*This book wouldn't have turned out as great as it did if it wasn't for you two!*). Thank you Diana Nightingale, Earl Nightingale's widow, for permission to reprint the work of Earl Nightingale's "The Strangest Secret". Thank you Mike McColgan and the Street Dogs for making music. Thank you Michael and Loren Iorio for introducing me to the Street Dogs music. Thank you Mike Martin for the 9/11/2011 Dropkick Murphys/Street Dogs/Stiff Little Fingers concert ticket. Thank you Howard Litwak. Thank you Rick Noel. Thank you Bob Fuhr, Adam Brown and Dan Silver. Thank you Ryan Pakenas. Thank You John Viscosi. Thank you Gareth Bobowski. Lastly, thank you to my family and friends for your love and support towards my writing projects, and also for your support and patronage towards the pizza place- I especially want to thank Aunt Sue, Aunt Lynda, Uncle Marc, Uncle Jim, Aunt Linda, Uncle John, as well as all of my Hallenbeck cousins.

Thank You for reading this book.

Also By The Author...

<u>Books authored by Chris Hallenbeck</u>

The Miraculous 54 Day Rosary Novena to Our Lady

...Now available in 5 different languages and 10 formats!...

<u>Books including Chris Hallenbeck as a contributing writer</u>

Hometown Sports Heroes, Vol 1.– 16 Classic Baseball Tales
By: Mike Hauser

Check out greatpointpublishing.com

End Notes

1. Barrett, Liz. *"The 2018 Pizza Power Report: A State of The Industry Analysis."* PMQ. Pizza Magazine.
   25 February 2019,
   www.pmq.com/December-2017/The-2018-Pizza-Power-Report-A-State-of-the-Industry-Analysis/

2. Vereckey, Betsy. "Worst jobs in America." *thestacker.com,*
   25 February 2019,
   thestacker.com/stories/1777/worst- jobs-america

3. "50 Best Jobs in America for 2019", *glassdoor.com,*
   25 February 2019,
   www.glassdoor.com/List/Best-Jobs-in-America-LST_KQ0,20.htm

4. Glassdoor Team. "Top Jobs for Sales Professionals",
   glassdoor.com, 21 February 2019,
   www.glassdoor.com/blog/top-jobs-for-sales-professionals/

5. Barrett, Liz. *"Pizza Power Report 2010."* PMQ Pizza
   Magazine, September 2010, Volume 14 Issue 7 : 56-64.

6. Brandau, Mark. "U.S. Restaurant Count Continues To Fall".
   Nation's Restaurant News. 3 September 2012.
   www.nrn.com/article/us-restaurant-count-continues-fall

7. Nightingale, Earl/Diana. The Strangest Secret. Keys
   Publishing, Inc. 1956/1996. www.earlnightingale.com

8. Bettger. Frank. How I Raised Myself From Success In Selling.
   Prentice Hall Press. New York. 1986. Pages III, 34-37.

9. Litwak, Howard. "About Me". www.howardlitwak.com
   September 29, 2014.

10. Litwak, Howard. Personal Email Interview.
    5 December 2012.

11. Noel, Rick. Personal Email Interview. 5 October 2014.

12. "Williamsburg, Virginia." *Wikipedia.com,* 14 August 2018. en.wikipedia.org/wiki/Williamsburg, Virginia

13. "Explore Colonial Williamsburg" 14 August 2018. www.colonialwilliamsburg.com/explore?from=homedefault

14. "Things to do in Williamsburg." *Tripadvisor.com,* 14 August 2018. www.tripadvisor.com/Attractions-g58313-Activities-Williamsburg Virginia.html

15. "Colonial Williamsburg." *Tripadvisor.com,* 14 August 2018. www.tripadvisor.com/Attraction Review-g58313-d102549-Reviews-Colonial Williamsburg WilliamsburgVirginia.html

16. Taylor, April. "Bridge to The 18th Century." *Daily Press.,* 11 August 2018. articles.dailypress.com/2003-01-25/news/0301250222 1 pedestrian-bridge-colonial-williamsburg-s-visitor-center-historic-area

17. Fuhr, Bob. "Facebook Profile." *Facebook,* 11 August 2018. www.facebook.com/bob.fuhr.3

18. "Bob Fuhr." *Linkedin.com,* 14 August 2018. www.linkedin.com/in/bob-fuhr-37802a1

19. "Gerry Spence." *Wikipedia.com,* 14 August 2018. en.wikipedia.org/wiki/Gerry Spence

20. "Gerry Spence." *Gerryspence.com,* 14 August 2018. gerryspence.com/

21. "A Trial Lawyer Must Be a Good Storyteller." *The Law Offices of Barton Morris,* 14 August 2018, michigancriminalattorney.com/trial-lawyer-storyteller/

22. Meyer, Philip. <u>Storytelling For Lawyers</u>., Oxford University Press. 2014. Pages 39-40.

23. "Altercasting." *Wikipedia.com,* 11 August 2018. https://en.wikipedia.org/wiki/Altercasting

24. Bernstein, Elizabeth. "If You Want to Persuade People, Try 'Altercasting'." *The Wall Street Journal. 6 September 2016.*

25. Allen, Pam. "Capital City Gastropub general manager buys into new title: owner". Albany Business Review. 9 August 2018. www.bizjournals.com/albany/blog/2013/05/capital-city-gastropub-general-manager.html

26. Capital City Gastropub. "About Us". 9 August 2018. www.capcitygastropub.com/about-us

27. Capital City Gastropub. "Finding the perfect beer to pair with a meal takes the dining experience to another level. We offer a large selection of craft beers made by some of the most renowned breweries worldwide." *Facebook,* 21 July 2018, 8:19a.m., www.facebook.com/CapitalCityGastropub/

28. "5 Best Burger Places in Albany". 9 August 2018. www.1broadwayalbany.com/albany-new-york/5-best-burger-places-in-albany/

29. Kavarana, Zarah. "Here's where to get the best brunch in Albany." Hudson Valley Magazine. 9 August 2018. www.hvmag.com/Your-Guide-Where-to-Get-the-Best-Brunch-Spots-in-Albany/

30. Bovee, Joshua. "Devil Daves breaks new ground." The Leader Herald. 9 August 2018. www.leaderherald.com/news/local-news/2018/06/devil-daves-breaks-new-ground/

31. Rader, Dusten. "Spicy Solution: Devil Dave's makes Bloody Marys easy." The Fulton County Express. 9 August 2018. www.fultoncountyexpress.com/spicy-solution-devil-daves- makes-bloody-marys-easy/

32. Pakenas, Ryan. "Well, we picked up our first Airline. Private Company just purchased. Works for me." *Facebook,* 14 March 2018, 11:41a.m., www.facebook.com/Ryan.Pakenas

33. Pakenas, Ryan. "Facebook Chat interview." *Facebook,* 13 July 2018, 12:27p.m., www.facebook.com/Ryan.Pakenas

34. Pakenas, Ryan. "Who dat? All up in the interewebs!" *Facebook,* 24 May 2018, 22:07p.m., www.facebook.com/Ryan.Pakenas

35. Friedman, Ann. "Bloody Mary sticks are a devilishly clever idea." *The Daily Gazette,* 9 August 2018 dailygazette.com/article/2018/03/05/bloody-mary-sticks-a-devilishly-clever-idea

36. "About Devil Daves Bloody Mary Sticks.", *devilddaves.com,* 17 September 2018, devildaves.com/pages/about-devil-daves-bloody-mary-sticks

37. "James Jamerson." *Wikipedia.com,* 11 August 2018. en.wikipedia.org/wiki/James Jamerson#Jamerson's equipment

38. DeSantis, Vincent. Toward Civic Integrity: Re-establishing the Micropolis. The Troy Book Makers. Troy, NY. 2007. Pages 31, 32, 35, 36

39. McMartin, Barbara. Hides, Hemlocks, and Adirondack History: How The Tanning Industry Influenced the Region's Growth. North Country Books. Utica, NY. 1992. Page 11

40. McMartin, Barbara with W. Alec Reid. The Glove Cities: How people and their craft built two cities. Lake View Press. Caroga, NY. 1999. Page 23

41. Conwell, Russel with Robert Shackleton. <u>Acres of Diamonds</u>. Great Point Publishing. Gloversville, NY. 2019. Pages 2, 39, 40,42, 180, 196.

42. "Russel Conwell." *Wikipedia.com,* 28 February 2019. en.wikipedia.org/wiki/RussellConwell#"AcresofDiamonds"

43. Trebay, Guy. "Heir to a Glove Town's Legacy", *The New York Times*, 21 October 2009. <u>www.nytimes.com/2009/10/22/fashion/22GLOVERSVILLE.html?_r=2&emc=eta1&pagewanted=all</u>

44. Ziglar, Zig. <u>Ziglar on Selling</u>. Thomas Nelson. Nashville. 1991. Pages xiv

45. "Deacon Jones." *Wikipedia.com,* 22 April 2019. https://en.wikipedia.org/wiki/Deacon Jones

46. "Deacon Jones." *Azqoutes.com,* 22 April 2019. https://www.azquotes.com/author/30623 Deacon Jones

47. Street Dogs. "Fighter." *Street Dogs.*, Hellcat., 2010, track 17.

Made in the USA
Middletown, DE
31 July 2020